THE GOLDEN BOOK OF
POLAND

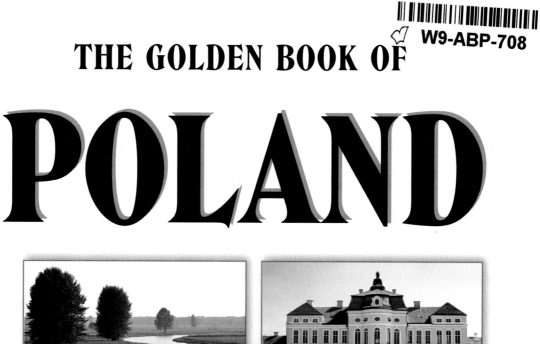

Written by
GRZEGORZ RUDZIŃSKI

Photographs by
PAWEŁ HERZOG

BONECHI - GALAKTYKA

ISBN: 83-89896-29-X

Project and editorial conception: Casa Editrice Bonechi
Publication Manager: Monica Bonechi
Graphic design: Sonia Gottardo

Text: Grzegorz Rudziński
Translation: Alicja Cendrowska
Photographs: Paweł Herzog
Editor: Piotr Staroń
Proofreader: Krzysztof Chętko

Photos on pages 8 (down), 9, 10, 11, 98, 99, 100, 101, 102 (top), 103
and back cover photo are taken from the Archives of Casa Editrice Bonechi.
Photo on page 95 (top left) was taken by Arturo Mari, Osservatore Romano.

Photos on pages 18, 19, 20, 21 and 30 (top) were taken by J. F. Kluczyńscy
Photos on pages 23, 24, 25 and 31 (bottom) were taken by Jacek Wojtas
Photo of Pope John Paul II on page 102 - was taken by Piotr Tumidajski / FotoKAI
Photos on page 126 were taken by Tomasz Gmerek

Cover photos: top left: Cracow
                   top right: Malbork
                   bottom left: Gdansk
                   bottom right: Warsaw. Royal Castle
Back cover: Warsaw, Łazienki, Palace on Water

Printed in Italy by Centro Stampa Editoriale Bonechi.

Introduction

Poland stretches over an area situated in the geometrical centre of Europe between the Baltic Sea and the northern slopes of the Carpathians and the Sudetes. This land mass is 312,685 km², and the Vistula and Odra are its main rivers. The country shares borders with Germany, the Czech Republic, Slovakia, Ukraine, Belarus, Lithuania, and in the north with the Kaliningrad District of Russia and also with Denmark via the territorial sea. Warsaw, situated on the middle Vistula, now functions as the capital city, however historically, several other cities proudly carried that name.

The Polish landscape is predominantly lowland: the Podlaska, Mazovian, Wielkopolska and Silesian lowlands are utilised as farmland interspersed with both large and small patches of forest. Areas of tourist interest are spread evenly across the whole country. Beaches covered with quartzite powdery sand in shades ranging from white to light beige stretch along the northern coastline. The scenic beauty of the ever choppy Baltic and the possibility of finding amber – the gold of the north, compensate the lack of any guarantee of 100 per cent sunny weather. Further south, the landscape becomes dotted with serene lakes, which constitute a wide belt of lake lands. The lowlands of central Poland are densely populated even though large cities are as common here as large forests. In Warsaw's immediate neighbourhood lies the Kampinos Forest *(Puszcza Kampinoska)*, and in the region of Łódź, a city with a population of nearly a million, there are the Bolimów and the Pilica forests *(Puszcza Bolimowska, Puszcza Pilicka)*. Below Poznań, there lies the Wielkopolski National Park featuring lakes and forests with clusters of ancient oak-trees. The Silesian Lowland, the most south-reaching, climbs rapidly by several hundred metres and joins the Sudetes. The highest peak of these old mountains is Śnieżka (1602 m) belonging to the Karkonosze range stretching along the border with the Czech Republic. South-East Poland comprises of picturesque uplands and lush vegetation of the northern slopes of the Carpathians. The Lubelska Upland is characterised by a warm summer and atmospheric landscapes. The area of the Małopolska Upland is divided by the not so high but very scenic Świętokrzyskie Mountains, and the Cracow-Wieluń Upland is in itself a range of miniature mountains with fantastically shaped Jurassic rocks. The Silesian Upland has been nearly completely urbanised, but the close proximity to the Carpathians redeems the environmental situation of this multimillion agglomeration. This mountain range retains much of its natural beauty and stretches latitudinally along the whole of the Polish-Slovak border. Its highest cluster – the Tatras, lays claims to be the largest area of alpine wildlife between the Alps and the Caucasus. At 2499 m the northern mountaintop of Mt Rysy is the highest peak of the Polish Tatras. Poland has 23 national parks out of which the Biebrza *(Biebrzański Park Narodowy)* is the largest and covers impassable

The spearhead of St. Maurice spear (10th century copy). The German Emperor Otto III handed over the spear to Bolesław Chrobry in Gniezno in 1000.

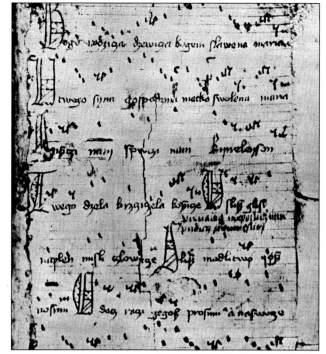

"Bogurodzica", the oldest Polish anonymous religious hymn, dates back to the 13th century. It was a religious hymn sang by the Polish knights riding into battle. The legend says that St. Wojciech was the author of "Bogurodzica". The medieval manuscript from 1407.

bogs, sometimes called the European Amazonia. The oldest of parks, the Białowieża *(Białowieski Park Narodowy)*, untouched by an axe, is the only remaining lowland forest on the continent, and which up until World War I sheltered the last free-living European bison. Though on the brink of extinction, the species was saved thanks to a breeding programme, and today they can be found in several places in Poland.

Despite many wars, Poland has been left rich in historical sites, mostly in cities, but it is not uncommon to encounter little pearls of architecture in rural areas. The beginnings of human settlements on Polish territory date much further back than the origins of Polish statehood. During the Neolithic age, in the Świętokrzyskie Mountains, there was a flint-mining centre for tool production purposes. In the Bronze Age, most of the land was dominated by tribes of the Lusatian culture, who built fortified settlements encircled by walls made of earth and wood. A reconstruction of one of those structures can be found at Biskupin. In the period of cultural exchange with the Roman Empire, a trade route called the Amber Road traversed Polish territory. Supratribal communities started to occur in the eighth century. Gradually, the Polanie tribe with their capital in Gniezno started to play the most important role. The oldest records mention the rule of Mieszko of the Piast dynasty. In 966, by marrying Dubravka, a Christian Czech princess, the Duke adopted Christianity and introduced his people into the orbit of Latin civilization. His male descendants ruled in

Poland until 1370, in Mazovia until 1526, and in Silesia until 1675. Mieszko's female descendants can be traced among the Polish royalty as far as 1795. Mieszko's son, Bolesław I Chrobry furnished Poland with the first martyr when he sent bishop Wojciech to pagan Prussia on a peace mission in 997. Two years later after the missionary's death, Wojciech was announced the first saint patron of Poland (St Adalbert). The second person to be beatified was Stanisław, bishop of Cracow, who had been slain in 1079 when trying to oppose the injustice of King Bolesław II Śmiały. The legend of the first saint has implanted in the Polish consciousness respect for action without the use of violence, the second one the conviction of the right to oppose the authorities.

Between 1138 and 1295, Poland underwent a process of feudal fragmentation and the weakening of the centralised power base of Cracow. It was also a period of dynamic economic growth, although harvests were plundered by the Mongols in 1241. Earlier, in 1226, Duke Konrad of Mazovia appealed to the Teutonic Knights to help him defend his realm against Prussian and Lithuanian invasions. The situation in the country changed with the return of centralised monarchy at the turn of the 13th century. Most importantly, the Teutonic Knights turned into foes. Władysław Łokietek fought a winning battle against them (Płowce, 1332), however, this did not change the odds. Casimir the Great (the founder of the University of Cracow in 1364) took them to the papal court and managed to regain some of the land, which the

4

"The Castle", Bernardo Bellotto caled Canaletto, View of Krakowskie Przedmieście from the Sigismundus Column 1767-1768.

Teutonic Order had annexed, but it was not until the Polish-Lithuanian alliance that their lawlessness was brought to an end. After the death of childless Casimir the Great (1370), his nephew, Louis of Hungary ascended the throne (Polish-Hungarian friendship has many far-reaching sources), and after him, his daughter, Jadwiga, who reigned between 1384 and 1399. In 1386, she married the Grand Duke Jagiełło of Lithuania, who christened himself Władysław. Jadwiga died widely revered by the populace (she was canonised in 1997). Thanks to her generosity, Władysław refurbished the university, which since then has been called "Jagiellonian". In 1410, together with the Lithuanians, Władysław crushed the Teutonic Knights in the battle of Grunwald. His son Kazimierz Jagiellończyk reaped the political fruit of this battle, when he reclaimed Gdansk in 1466, and his grandson Sigismund the Old, who made Albrecht Hohenzollern, the Grand Master of the Order, his liegeman.

The political system that evolved in Poland throughout the 15th century was known as the Nobles' Democracy. The rule *neminem captivabimus* protected Polish *szlachta* (gentry or nobility) from lawless arrest. In fact, the king became a constitutional monarch. The *nihil novi* act transferred all legislative power from the king to the *Sejm* (the chamber of envoys at the parliament). In the days of the Reformation, the strong position of citizens against the monarch nullified the rule *cuius regio eius religio*, and thus Poland enjoyed guarantees of religious tolerance. The 17th century, a Golden Age for Poland, ended with the reign of Sigismund III Vasa, who embroiled Poland with Sweden for 70 years and with Russia for centuries. The country fell into decline. Yet in 1683, King Jan III Sobieski still managed to overpower a vast Turkish army in Vienna. However, his successor was no longer able to rule without foreign protection. The anarchy of the *szlachta*, the degeneration of towns, and wars put Poland on a downward course straight into the arms of Tsar Peter the Great. Attempts to restore sovereignty (Confederation of Bar 1768-72 and the Great Sejm 1788-92) ended with a Russian-German pact that sealed the partitioning of Poland. The struggle for independence over the following 123 years culminated in the chaos of World War I, out of which emerged the multiethnic *Druga Rzeczpospolita* (Second Commonwealth). Twenty years of interwar independence augmented Poland against erasure from the maps of Europe by the Stalin-Hitler pact of 1939-41, and the Yalta decree, which handed the country over to the Soviets. Between 1944 and 1989, Poland was part of the Eastern Bloc. In 1978, Karol Wojtyła, the archbishop of Cracow, became the Pope. In 1980 Polish workers created a trade union known as Solidarity and by opposing the authorities, they peacefully overturned the system. The fall of the Soviet Union finished the task. In 1992, the last Russian military unit left Poland. Soon, the country joined NATO, and since 2004 Poland has been a member state of the European Union.

Warsaw. View of the Old Town and the Castle Square from the bell tower of the academic Church of St Ann.

Warsaw (Warszawa)

The Polish capital city is located centrally on the Mazovian Lowland on the middle Vistula. It is the biggest city in Poland and forms the second largest urban settlement. The number of its inhabitants exceeds 1,700,000.

Apart from its political and administrative functions it is also a very important industrial, academic and artistic centre. Interesting historical sites and museums make it a vibrant tourist destination. The emblem of the city is a mermaid, a character from the legend of Warsz, who was allegedly the first landholder on the Vistula escarpment, from where the city evolved.

The oldest human dwellings in this area were the fishing and farming settlements dating from the 10th and 11th century. Towards the end of the 13th century, during a period of political independence in Mazovia, the local dukes built a stronghold on the spot where today the Royal Castle is located. In the vicinity of the castle

developed a town called Warszewa (the name used until the 17th century) and was granted a settlement right around the year 1300. The first significant event in Warsaw was a papal trial of 1339, which had to settle a dispute between Casimir the Great and the Teutonic Order. Despite the disadvantageous location on a high escarpment, the settlement flourished thanks to the trade on the Vistula – the major transportation route of the time. By the 15th century, Warsaw outgrew Płock, the ancient capital of Mazovia, and took over its administrative functions. In 1526, after the death of the last Mazovian duke, Janusz III, Warsaw along with the whole Mazovia was annexed to Poland and soon gained in political importance. The castle underwent extension works as ordered by King Sigismund August and was frequented by his sister Anna Jagiellonka. Since 1569, Warsaw was the gathering place of the general parliamentary convention (*sejm walny*), and from 1573 all royal elections took place there (the political system of old Poland more

View of the Royal Castle from Krakowskie Przedmieście St.

Monument to King Sigismund III Vasa, erected in the Castle Square at the order of his son Władysław IV.

closely resembled a republic than a monarchy: kings were elected through a public vote for a lifelong tenure. The throne was not hereditary, but royal sons were often elected as successors). After the fire at Cracow Castle in 1596, King Sigismund III Vasa moved to Warsaw and the royal administration soon followed suit in 1611. Despite the fact that coronation ceremonies always took place in Cracow, it is officially accepted that Warsaw has been the capital of Poland since 1596. The inhabitants of Warsaw pay due respect to the so-called Sigismund's Column, the monument dedicated to the king who achieved little else that is noteworthy except for this court relocation. The wars with Sweden, brought about due to his stubborn insistence on holding onto both crowns, led to the first devastation of the city some 25 years after his death. Even though the next century (1660-1760) did not prove to be the total ruin of Warsaw (1677 is the year of the construction of the royal residence in Wilanów, in 1740 Stanisław Konarski founded Collegium Nobilium, and in 1747 Załuski brothers opened the first public library), the city had to wait until 1764 and the reign of Stanisław August Poniatowski for a return to the good times.

Warsaw. Old Town Square with the Mermaid Statue relocated here from its previous position on the city walls.

Royal Castle in Warsaw.
Chapel of August III Poniatowski in the King's suite.

Warsaw became the centre of intellectual life. It saw the publishing of periodicals and the opening of Szkoła Rycerska, a military school for cadets. Thanks to the king's patronage of the arts, the Royal Castle and the Palace on the Water (the king's summer residence) were frequented by the most enlightened minds for the so-called Thursday Lunches. A permanent theatre scene was also established. During the Kościuszko Insurrection in 1794, the Russian army stormed right-bank Warsaw (called Praga) and slaughtered the inhabitants. Between the years 1795 and 1806, under the Prussian government, the city experienced an economic recession. In 1807, Napoleon Bonaparte created the puppet Duchy of Warsaw, and in 1815 Tsar Alexander crowned himself in

Houses in Krakowskie Przedmieście, reconstructed with all details from the paintings of Bellotto.

Holy Cross Church in Krakowskie Przedmieście, a Baroque place of worship and the burial place of Frédéric Chopin's heart.

Warsaw Cathedral as the king of Poland. A year later, the University of Warsaw was founded. Over the next hundred years, despite several suppressed uprisings, Poland still played a role in the 19th century industrial revolution. Between 1845 and 1848 a railway was built connecting Warsaw with Vienna and later with St Petersburg in 1862. During World War I, the city was occupied by the Germans. In August 1920, the Bolshevik offensive stopped at Warsaw's doorstep. The year 1921 saw the opening of the airport and in 1926 the first radio station began broadcasting. In 1939 Warsaw had a population of approximately 1.3 million out of which 400 thousand were Jews. The events of World War II literally swept the whole city away. The first major fires

Warsaw – Wilanów. Baroque palace of King Jan III Sobieski.

and bombing took place in September 1939 during the siege of Warsaw. During the city's occupation, the Germans introduced a system of extermination of the Jewish population (the Ghetto Uprising of 1943 was no longer about survival, but about honourable death), and a system of terror against the Poles: executions of hostages, a curfew, and the liquidation of all cultural life. In the summer of 1944, the Polish underground Home Army, or Armia Krajowa, started the Warsaw Uprising (01/08-02/10/1944) in order to reclaim the city from the German occupants. Lack of support from the Red Army stationed on the left bank of the Vistula (Russia was officially an ally of Poland) and the German reprisal led to the wiping out of 84 per cent of the city's resources and the death of 800 thousand people. The post-war years saw the restoration of historical sites, many of which were reconstructed from the surviving paintings of Bernardo Bellotto, an Italian artist who worked in Warsaw in the 18th century (known in Poland as Canaletto, after taking on the name of his famous uncle).

◀ *Palace on the Water in Łazienki. King Stanisław August Poniatowski's favourite summer residence.*

Socialist-realist Palace of Culture and Science, popularly known as PeKiN.

11

Żelazowa Wola. Birthplace of Frédéric Chopin.

Żelazowa Wola

The village is located on the outskirts of Sochaczew, some fifty kilometres west of Warsaw. The word *wola* (will) in the place name is semantically related to the concept of freedom and hints at the origins of the village, which is an example of how territories used to be colonised in medieval times, i.e. settlers were relocated to unpopulated areas in exchange for a few years of tax exemption. However, the oldest

Żelazowa Wola. Patio outside the Music Room.

mention is from 1579, when it was in the hands of the brothers: Mikołaj and Piotr Żelazo. At the beginning of the 19th century, the village belonged to the Skarbek family, and it was here that Nicholas Chopin, a Frenchman living in Poland since 1787, found employment as a tutor. In 1806 he married Justyna Krzyżanowska, and

four years later on 1st March 1810 (though the birth certificate states 22nd February) a son was born – Fryderyk – a child prodigy, and soon the most famous Polish composer.

The foundation of a museum in Żelazowa Wola at the end of the 19th century commemorated this event. The idea was realised thanks to the collective efforts of the Russian composer Mily Balakirev, who initiated the erection of the first statue of Chopin in 1894, and the Polish virtuoso Ignacy Jan Paderewski. The conversion work in the annex of the manor (miraculously saved from two fires) did not start until 1926 under the instruction of Mieczysław Kuzma. Also around that time, Franciszek Krzywda-Polkowski creat-

Nieborów. Tympanum of Radziwiłł's Palace.

Nieborów. View of the park next to the palace.

Lion guarding the driveway to the palace in Nieborów.

Arkadia and Nieborów

Some 25 kilometres south-west of Sochaczew, in close proximity to the Bolimów Forest, two sites of the highest artistic, historic and academic importance can be found. The Romantic park in Arkadia and the palace and park complex in Nieborów both feature on the national heritage list.

The palace in Nieborów today houses a branch of the National Museum and is one of the best preserved magnate residencies in Poland. It was built between 1690 and 1696 by an accomplished architect Tylman van Gameren for Michał Radziejowski, the archbishop of Gniezno. Under the ownership of the Radziwiłł family, a collection of practical objects, pieces of art and an excellent library was accrued between the years 1774 and 1945. Behind the palace, a park was laid out and divided into sections representing the French and the English style. It must have proven too small for the palace own-

ed the beautiful park surrounding the manor (seven hectares of land with an original arrangement of trees, bushes and smaller architectural features). The existence of the museum was not inaugurated properly until after World War II. Soon after that, the museum became an active centre for cultivating Chopin's music. Summer recitals have been held here every Sunday between May and September since 1954 and attract Polish and foreign musicians, including laureates of the International Fryderyk Chopin Piano Competition. On Saturdays during July and August the concert tunes of young performers fill the air. During the season of 2004, the place was visited by over sixty musician-participants from China, Finland, France, Japan, Germany, Poland, Russia and the US. In addition to musically gifted young people, there were also such well-established celebrities as Regina Smendzianka and Piotr Paleczny. The forthcoming concert seasons look very promising too.

Arkadia. Romantic buildings in Radziwiłł's park.

Architectural park's elements in the form of aqueduct.

Mazovia (Mazowsze)

ers, because towards the end of the 18th century a decision was made to create a romantic park in Arkadia situated five kilometres away. Helena Radziwiłł, the lady of Nieborów, chose for its location the banks of the Skierniewka River, which naturally forms here two picturesque ponds. The park is full of Antique and Gothic styled structures: Diana's Temple, the Aqueduct, Archpriest's Sanctuary, Margrave House, the Gothic House and others. It would be worthwhile to combine the trip to Arkadia and Nieborów with a ramble in the nearby Bolimów Forest *(Puszcza Bolimowska)* inhabited by fallow deer. The river Rawka, which cuts through the heart of the forest, is protected as a nature reserve.

Attractive tourist sites, ideal for one-day trips from the capital, can be found on the seasonally changing Mazovian plains within the environs of Warsaw. There are so many of these sites that, in fact, one could dedicate a whole new book to them. One will find here medieval castles, churches ranging from Romanesque to contemporary styles, palaces and manor houses, impenetrable forests and clear rivers unspoilt by the industrial revolution. There are sites evoking memories of great Poles such as the house of the Nobel Prize Winner Władysław Reymont situated in Lipce, or the surviving country manor of the Skarbek family – the birthplace of Frédéric Chopin.

Łowicz. Interior of the cathedral.

Łowicz

Łowicz is the nearest urban centre from Arkadia and Nieborów. Marvellous examples of sacred architecture date back to a time when the town was in the hands of the Gniezno archbishops. In 1815, the land was taken over by the Russian tsars, and in the aftermath of the

Ethnographic exhibition in Łowicz Museum.

marriage of tsarevitch Constantine and Joanna Grudzińska turned into the Duchy of Łowicz. The autonomy of the Łowicz province under the bishops' protection and later during partitions allowed for a growth of a culture particular only to this area. It is still apparent in the regional costume, the decorative arts: Łowicz stripes *(pasiaki łowickie)*, the dialect and some particularly elaborate celebrations (e.g. Corpus Christi). The region of Łowicz belongs to the best preserved areas of living folklore in Europe. The new administrative division of the Catholic Church drafted during the pontificate of John Paul II gave Łowicz the status of a capital of the diocese. Its major tourist attractions are the aforementioned churches full of interesting sculptures and paintings, as well as the ethnographic park, the castle ruins and the branch of the National Museum, exhibiting a collection of folklore art which will fascinate not only ethnographers. Many villages around Łowicz are inhabited by folk craftsmen: pot makers, blacksmiths, weavers and creators of cut-outs. The latter is particularly characteristic for this region: colourful paper cut-outs used to serve as decorations for the house interiors, but today are more of a collector's curiosity.

15

Płock. Panorama of the Tumskie Hill across the Vistula.

Płock

The first capital of Mazovia and the oldest town of the region is situated on a cliff high over the Vistula some 130 kilometres downriver from Warsaw. In the period from 1079 to 1138, it functioned as an unofficial capital of Poland and the seat of the ruling princes: Władysław Herman and his son Bolesław Krzywousty. The second phase in the town's growth came in the 16th century during which time the cathedral underwent some restoration and restructuring works. With the opening of a huge petrochemical plant in the 20th century, Płock became one of the major industrial centres in the country.

From the many historical buildings, Płock can boast a cathedral basilica: built in masonry between 1126 and 1141, initially Romanesque and later adapted to the Renaissance style by Italian architects working in Poland.

Romanesque cathedral in Płock.

A stone sarcophagus held in the southern tower since 1825 contains the coffins of Herman and Krzywousty. The cast bronze atrium doors are a copy of the famous Romanesque doors, *(Drzwi Płockie)*, ordered around 1154 by a Polish duke, Bolesław Kędzierzawy, to be made in Magdeburg and presented to the Cathedral of St Sophia in Novgorod the Great. Opposite the cathedral, there is a building formed from the walls of the former Benedictine Abbey and from the remains of the castle of King Casimir the Great. Today it functions as the Museum of Mazovia housing the best collection of Art Nouveau in Poland. The Diocesan Museum, on the other hand, boasts a unique display of silk and gold woven belts from the 17th and 18th century. In historical times, they were an indispensable element of male finery for the nobles (*szlachta*).

"Drzwi Płockie", a fragment.

Grabarka – the Holy Mountain. A forest of crosses.

Orthodox shrine.

Grabarka

Podlasie, Masuria and Warmia are regions lying east and
north of Mazovia. They are sometimes called "the green
lungs" of Poland and their natural beauty is recognised
on a European scale. Podlasie stretches up to the eastern
border and has four national parks protecting the total
area of 92,000 hectares. With traditions dating back to
the times of the First Commonwealth (*Pierwsza Rzeczpospolita*), it is also a multicultural region, where people
of Catholic, Muslim and Orthodox faith have coexisted
for centuries. An important place of worship for the latter group is the Holy Mountain of Grabarka, which is situated very near to the border checkpoint in Połowce. Its
slopes are covered by a forest of crosses put up around
the Orthodox Church as an expression of prayers for
God's grace. A cross dedicated to a plea would be made
at home and then carried on the shoulders to the Holy
Mountain.

Białowieża. An old forest lodge.

Bison (Bison bonasus).

Białowieski National Park

Stretching across the Polish border, the Białowieski Forest *(Puszcza Białowieska)* conceals in its heart the Białowieża National Park, protecting the last remains of the primeval European forest, which used to cover most of the continent some thousand years ago. The park was founded in 1921 and for thirty years remained the only dwelling place of the European bison *(żubr)*. The species was nearly wiped out in the 18th century and survived only here and in the Caucasus. The starvation brought about by World War I led to the extinction of the last free living specimens. The replenishing of the species is a tremendous success of the park's employees. Zoo animals were brought to Białowieża and a new herd was recreated within a special croft by means of breeding techniques and a lot of patience. By 1952, the herd had become large enough to allow for the setting free of the first few animals. Apart from the bison, the park is inhabited by other rare species: wolf, lynx, otter, beaver, white-tailed eagle and crane. The richness and diversity of the plant life is also an important feature of the park: it encompasses 20 types of forest.

19

Meanders of the Biebrza.

Biebrzański National Park

Naturalists had long been commenting on the unique qualities of the region, before the largest national park was finally created in 1993. It encompasses 263 bird species, (185 of which have their nesting grounds here), 47 mammals and numerous species of insects. Vascular plants are represented by 872 species, although the number of types of mushroom, moss and lichen has not been quantified. Larger mammals are represented by: moose, deer, roe deer, wild boar, wolf, lynx, otter, and beaver. There are also many birds: white-tailed eagle, golden eagle, crane, egret, and of course white stork. Regrettably, as many as 21 different bird species are threatened with extinction, but the park gives them a chance of preservation. For example: out of the 250 nests of the Montagu's harrier, which remain in Central Europe, 72 are sheltered in the Biebrza bogs. From the total 59,223 hectares of park territory only 26 per cent is covered by forest. The majority of land comprises of impassable peat bogs and marshes running for 160 km along the course of the Biebrza River. The layer of peat in the river's valley is several metres deep. Since it is the only wild and unregulated river on the continent, ecologists see the Biebrza plant life and geomorphologic formations as an ideal example of a natural river basin. Twice along the river's course, in places called Red Marsh *(Czerwone Bagno)* and Ławka Marsh *(Bagno Ławki)*, the valley becomes 20 kilometres wide. The river itself is the major tourist route across the Park and is often used for kayaking. In 1996, the area on the Narew river, above the point where the Biebrza joins it, was turned into the Narew National Park.

Moose (Alces alces).

Święta Lipka. Baroque organ screen in the Jesuit Church.

Święta Lipka. Church facade.

Święta Lipka

On the border of the historical region of Warmia and among the northern forests and lakes of the Masurian Lake District, lies one of the most precious examples of Baroque architecture in Poland. It is the church in Święta Lipka *(Holy Lime Tree)* near Kętrzyn built in 1687-93 and a slightly more recent Jesuit monastery. The temple is surrounded by a sculpted rectangular cloister. Both structures were built for use by pilgrims, who have been arriving here at least since the 15th century.

The location of the church is related to the legend of a prisoner locked in the Kętrzyn Castle, who carved out an effigy of the Holy Virgin in a piece of lime tree while awaiting his execution. When the judges found it, they took it as a sign of God's grace and pardoned him. Freed again, the prisoner placed the figure on a wayside lime tree (the origin of the place name) and soon the site became known for its miraculous properties. The church interior is rich with decorations including the paintings of Maciej J. Meyer and a beautiful organ screen. The organ itself, constructed in the 17th century, has kept many characteristics of a Baroque instrument, even though at the beginning of the 20th century, new pipes were added giving it a more Romantic sound. It is one of the most exquisite instruments in Poland. Feliks Nowowiejski (1877-1946), one of the greatest Polish composers of the first half of the 20th century (next to Karol Szymanowski and Aleksander Tansman), used to play it in his youth (between 1887 and 1893) as a student of a famous Jesuit school built next to the monastery in 1722.

Olsztyn. Panorama of the historic city centre – the north view.

Olsztyn

The biggest city of Warmia (approximately 180,000 inhabitants) is today the capital of the Masuria-Warmia province and an important industrial and, in more recent times, academic centre. It has become one of the most significant tourist destinations, not so much because of its well preserved historical sites (notwithstanding their value), but as a result of the proximity of a multitude of clear lakes and forests. The city has a theatre and a philharmonic orchestra. The major attraction is the castle, built originally in a Gothic style by Warmia bishops, and fortified and defended by Nicholas Copernicus himself in the 16th century. Outside its walls lies a famous amphitheatre staging a number of artistic events during the summer season. A legendary event of 1970s and 1980s to be held here was the festival of poetry and music: *Spotkania Zamkowe,* which was even more effective in bringing poetry to the young people of the time than the Ministry of Culture.

Olsztyn. View of the castle from a latter-day amphitheatre.

Olsztyn. Houses around the Town Square.

Elblag Canal (Kanał Elbląski)

Lock on the Elblag Canal.

Designed in 1837 and built between 1844 and 1872, it represents one of the most fascinating engineering period pieces in Central Europe. By joining a chain of lakes and utilising the upper course of the Drwęca river, the canal connects Ostróda with what was formerly a major sea harbour in Elblag. The whole route is over 70 kilometres long and the difference in water levels can reach 100 metres. This is overcome by means of a system of slipways and locks, the only such example in Europe.

The economic importance of the canal has diminished today (due to Elblag being cut off from international waters) however the tourist potential of the area makes it an attractive destination. A several hours long trip on a pleasure boat allows the visitors to enjoy the scenery of the west Masuria, particularly as it is seen from the elevations along which the boat is pulled.

Elblag Canal. A unique slide used for water transport.

Lidzbark Warmiński. Tower of the parish church.

Lidzbark Warmiński. Castle facade.

Lidzbark Warmiński

The Warmian bishopric is situated on the territory which used to belong to the Warmians tribe before it was conquered by the Teutonic Knights. The diocese was created by the papal bull of 29th July 1243 issued by the Pope Innocent IV. The Treaty of Toruń in 1466 annexed Warmia to the Polish territory, but left the bishops with executive powers, such as the right to call for the local assembly *(sejmik)*. In the 16th century, Lidzbark Warmiński, the second biggest town of the diocese, became the seat of the bishops' court. Military offensives, which took place in 1703-1704 and 1944-1945, led to the destruction of the majority of the town's historic heritage. Today, it has nearly 20,000 inhabitants and is a centre of the food manufacturing industry. Nevertheless, it still boasts a few sites worth a visit. The biggest attraction is the red-brick bishops' castle dating from 1355-41 with a beautiful multi tiered Gothic cloister running around the square courtyard. Nowadays, the castle rooms hold a museum. Also notable is the Gothic Church of SS Peter and Paul, which was rebuilt several times and conceals Rococo furnishings. Remains of the town's fortifications can still be found here: fragments of city walls and a Gothic front of the gate from 1470. The position of bishop was often held by outstanding intellectuals and artists, such as Łukasz de Watzenrode, the patron of Nicholas Copernicus (who lived here between 1503 and 1510); Jan Dantyszek, an exceptional Latin poet, the most accomplished Polish man of letters before Jan Kochanowski; Stanisław Hozjusz, a theologian and the chairman of the Trident Council; Marcin Kromer, a historiographer and geographer; Jan Stefan Wydżga and

Lidzbark Warmiński. Interior of the castle's chapel.

Andrzej Chryzostom Załuski, crown chancellors, and finally Ignacy Krasicki (1735-1801), the greatest Polish poet of the 18th century, the author of fables, mock-heroic poems and satires, which so accurately depicted Polish national characteristics. Evidently, the muse of the bishop-poet must have survived within the walls of Lidzbark castle, as it does not cease to inspire the local organisers of the Lidzbark Festival of Humour and Satire.

In addition to having a friendly "muse", the castle is also said to be haunted. One can supposedly encounter a pair of glowing eyes belonging to a prisoner, who had been released from the castle dungeons in spite of his serious crimes. The legend says that he was blinded by the sun as he walked out into the courtyard.

Lidzbark Warmiński. Castle of the Warmia Bishops.

Frombork. Fortifications on the Cathedral Hill.

Frombork. Baroque altar in the cathedral.

Frombork

Frombork developed at the foot of the fortified Cathedral Hill at the end of the 13th century. It is situated on the slopes of the Elbląg Upland, at the point where the Warmia Lowland reaches the Vistula Lagoon. The town was granted municipal rights in 1310. The locals occupied themselves with trade, crafts and fishing. The history of the place abounded in dramatic events: wars and fires ravaged it repeatedly in 1414, 1455, 1520, 1626, 1703, 1772 and 1945. Despite all this, an outstanding cathedral, recalling the days when Nicholas Copernicus used to work there as a canon, has miraculously survived. This huge hall church was built between 1329 and 1388 in the Gothic style. It was dedicated to the Assumption of the Holy Virgin Mary and St Andrew. In the 15th century it was extended by the addition of the St George's Chapel (also called the Polish Chapel), and in the years 1732-35, the chapel of the Szembeks featuring Marcin Meyer's polychromies.

The furnishings of the cathedral belong to different periods. The main altar was made of colourful marble in 1750 by stonemasons from Dębnik near Cracow. Formerly, its place was occupied by a wooden pentaptych dating back to 1504, today located by the wall of the northern nave. St Bartholomew's altar, now standing near the sixth pillar in the southern nave, was given its current shape in 1633.

A hundred years earlier, Nicholas Copernicus was its custodian, and as the custom of the day demanded, his tomb was situated nearby. Copernicus lived in Frombork during the final stage of his life, which he devoted almost exclusively to astronomical observations and calculations. It was here that his magnum opus *De revolutionibus* acquired its final form. According to a legend of disputed accuracy, it was here in Frombork in 1543, that Copernicus received the first printed copy of his book on his deathbed.

Frombork. Gothic altar devastated in 1945.

Frombork. Detail of the cathedral's furnishings.

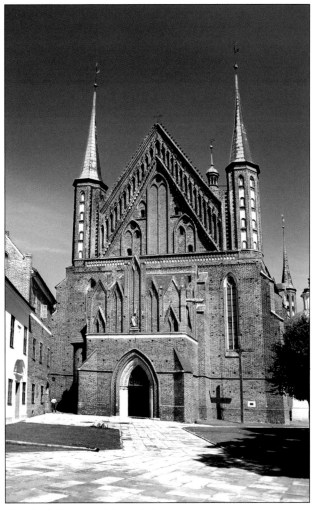

Frombork. Facade of the cathedral.

The cathedral's interior is adorned by an organ screen, concealing a Baroque instrument that was commissioned by the bishop Michał Radziejowski, (whose palace in Nieborów has already been mentioned). With its 4256 pipes divided into 61 scales, the sound of the instrument is highly regarded by performers of organ music.

Frombork. City walls with the gate and the Tower of Copernicus.

Frombork. Old Bishops' Palace.

27

Toruń. Gothic town hall.

Toruń

The city owes much of its fame and profits from tourism to the creator of the heliocentric theory, Nicholas Copernicus, who was born here in 1473. But had it not been a birthplace of anyone remarkable, it would still attract a lot of interest due to its outstanding beauty. Founded by the Teutonic Order in 1233, it soon became an important port on the Vistula and controlled most of the river trade. The town was a member of the Hanseatic League and developed dynamically until the end of the 17th century. In 1454, the local townspeople rejected Teutonic protection and offered the town to the Polish king. After 1793, the region found itself under Prussian domination and between 1807 and 1815 it was incorporated into the Duchy of Warsaw. It finally returned to Poland in 1918. World War II left Toruń relatively undamaged; however the attempt to Germanise the town by forcing Poles into

exile resulted in a population drop from 77,000 in 1938 to 15,000 in 1945.

Today, Toruń boasts the second largest complex of medieval architecture in Poland (after Cracow). It is also a significant industrial centre, which managed not to clash with its role as the most important tourist destination between Warsaw and Gdansk. Traditionally, it has always been famous for the production of delicious gingerbreads. Listed historic sites include the buildings and spatial organisation of the Old and New Town, the ruins of the Teutonic Knights' Castle as well as many other valuable structures, such as SS John the Baptist and John the Evangelist Church, the Cistercian monastic complex, the Franciscan monastic complex, the medieval Old Town Hall, the House under the Star and fragments of

Toruń. Statue of Nicholas Copernicus.

◄ *Toruń. Remains of the Teutonic Knights' castle with a tower.*

the city's fortifications including the Leaning Tower and the Gate near the Vistula river. Many visitors are attracted to the family house of Nicholas Copernicus at the meeting point of the Kopernika and Świętego Ducha streets, near the Monastic Gate. It is recommended to start the city sightseeing tour at the museum located in the Town Hall, and finish off with a walk along the Vistula and then across the bridge to the left bank. From this vantage point it is possible to admire one of the most picturesque urban panoramas in this part of the world.

Toruń's forts, the "latest" historic buildings of the city, have recently experienced more popularity with tourists. They were built between the years 1878 and 1914. Enthusiasts of 19th century fortifications can visit them by following a trail, which leads for 44 kilometres.

Ciechocinek. Production of salt from brine.

Ciechocinek. A clock of flowers in the heart of the spa.

Ciechocinek

Situated around 20 km south-east of Toruń, Ciechocinek is one of the most popular health spas in Poland. Since the end of the 18th century, salt has been technologically extracted on a large scale from the local brine spring. This was done by means of lifting water in a windmill contrap-tion and then filtering it through a twig tower. Vapours created during the process are known to have unique ther-apeutic qualities. Since 1836, drinking of the local miner-al water and partaking of thermal baths at the temperature of 38° C has also been highly recommended.

Golub-Dobrzyń

Golub-Dobrzyń. Castle.

In the 14th century, two towns: Polish Dobrzyń and Teutonic Golub were situated on the opposite banks of the Drwęca river, north-east of Toruń. After Poland reclaimed the Chełmno province, they were merged into one conurbation. The Teutonic Knights' castle in Golub, built in Gothic style between 1296 and 1308, was intercepted by Poles in 1454 and utilised as a royal castle. It was rebuilt in the 16th century with the addition of Renaissance architectural features: an attic and openwork turrets. Between the years 1603 and 1625, it served as a residence of the king's sister, Anna Wazówna, the protector of Protestants and the propagator of religious tolerance. Nowadays, it is the place where modern day knights' tournaments remind us of the medieval traditions of the place, and oratory competitions cultivate the art of debate.

The first modern Knight Tournament was held here in July 1977. Despite the fact that only five teams turned up at the approaches of the castle accepting the challenge, the tournament has become a regular event in the calendar of Golubsk's Branch of Polish Tourist Country-Lovers' Association (PTTK) and is the biggest tournament of medieval European art of fight in Poland today. The traditions of oratorical contests go back to 1971, when the first National Oratorical Contest for PTTK's tourist guides was organised thanks to the initiative of Zygmunt Kwiatkowski the director of Golubsk's Castel. Four years later high schools students were invited to participate in the contest and what is more from 1991 the International Oratorical Contest in Polish language has been held here annually.

Golub-Dobrzyń. Knights before the tournament.

Malbork

Rather a smallish city today, Malbork used to function as the capital of the Teutonic Order for 157 years. Reclaimed from the Teutonic Knights in 1466, it served as a seat of the Polish *starosta* (literally, "elder", an administrative official) until 1772. It remained under Prussian domination between the years 1772 and 1870, and then German between 1871 and 1945. Today it is known for its pasta factory and a massive medieval castle.

The construction of the stronghold began in 1277 with a bricked rectangle measuring 61 by 52 metres. Towards the end of the 13th century, it already had two towers: Klesza and Gdanisko. In 1309, Malbork received the status of a capital city. Among the ascetic buildings of the initial planning, more elaborate structures were created, such as the Palace of the Grand Master and the Great Dining Hall. The order was at

Malbork Castle. Detail of the Gothic well stonework.

the time expansionist and encroached on the Polish territory, which for centuries had embraced Christianity. In this context, the Christianising mission had no justification, however the idea of the crusade was still very much alive and the Order's ranks attracted knights from all over Europe. They found

Malbork.
Panorama of the Teutonic Knights' Castle
- view across the Nogat river.

Malbork Castle. Gothic courtyard with a cloister.

◄ *Malbork Castle. Palace of the Grand Master.*

accommodation in the purpose built building with the chapel of St Bartholomew. The earliest fortifications date back to the early 15th century, when the layout of the walls offered suitable protection against artillery fire. The Teutonic Order's significance began to fade from 1525 onwards after their Grand Master paid homage to the Polish king. The castle remained within Polish borders until 1772. It fell into ruin after Prussia took control of the region. Neither was the Gothic architecture valued by the Berlin elites. Since they considered the Sanssouci style to be the ideal of beauty, the castle soon became a source of cheap bricks. It was saved by the Romantics, who renewed

Malbork Castle. Example of an elaborate polychromic sculpture decoration.

the structure in accordance with their poetic ideals. The second attempt to rebuild the castle was founded more in technology and historical knowledge. It was conducted by Konrad Steinbrecht (until 1923) and Bernhard Schmid, who worked there until 1945. The third wave of reconstruction works was organised by the Poles, after the chaos of war had left only half of the complex standing. This undertaking started in the sixties with the immediate vicinity of the castle swept free of mines and cleaned up. The task was carried out successfully. In 1997, the castle was listed as a UNESCO World Heritage Site – the eighth to be designated in Poland.

Kashubia (Kaszuby)

Example of kashubian folk architecture gathered in the open-air museum in Wdzydze Kiszewskie.

This most northern region of Poland is also the most elevated area of the European Lowland. Wieżyca, the highest point of the Kashubian Lake District, lies at 328.6 m. Significant differences in heights and the presence of lakes bring to mind Switzerland. In fact, despite the lack of alpine landscapes, this part of Poland

▲ *Lake in the Kashubian Lake District.*

◄ *Example of kashubian folk architecture gathered in the open-air museum in Wdzydze Kiszewskie.*

◄ *Lake in the Kashubian Lake District.*

Examples of kashubian folk architecture gathered in the open-air museum in Wdzydze Kiszewskie.

is sometimes called the Kashubian Switzerland. It is an exceptionally picturesque region attractive for water sports lovers, fishermen, mushroom pickers (picking wild mushrooms is like a national sport for the Poles), hikers, cyclists and motorcyclists. Skiers benefit from severe winters and an abundance of hills. The slopes of Mt Wieżyca offer two types of ski lifts: a chair lift and a draglift. Geographically, Kashubia is also a very rewarding field for research, particularly for ethnographers and linguists. The folk culture of the region has many unique features. Its traditions can be observed during a visit to a heritage park in Wdzydze Kiszewskie. What can also be discerned here *in statu nascendi*, is the process of linguistic transformation of the inhabitants' speech. It evolved during the last millennium from East-Pomeranian dialects, so closely connected with the Polish language, into a separate literary tongue. Kashubians are the most northerly group of the Western Slavs, and their input into Polish cultural heritage is very significant. Józef Wybicki, the author of the Polish national anthem, came from Kashubia.

Example of kashubian folk architecture gathered in the open-air museum in Wdzydze Kiszewskie.

Richly embroidered traditional kashubian costume.

Gdansk. Old harbour basin on the Motława river illuminated by street lamps.

Gdansk (Gdańsk)

Archaeological findings of Arabic coins dating from the 8th and 9th century corroborate claims that in the early Middle Ages, in the area of today's Gdansk, there used to be a complex of strongholds whose inhabitants traded with faraway lands. In 997, at the order of the Duke of Poland, Bolesław Chrobry, the people were christened by the Prague bishop, Adalbert (Wojciech Sławnikowic). His mission in Prussia ended in martyrdom, and the story of his life (written in Rome in 999 after his canonisation) mentioned the name *gyddanyzc*. Linked with Poland in the 10th and 11th century, the city became a capital of a separate duchy in the 12th century. In 1186, Duke Sambor introduced the Cistercian Order to the nearby town of Oliwa, and his older brother, Świętopełk II the Great, strengthened the position of the duchy by gaining the Pope's protection. The last of his heirs, prince Mestwin, bequeathed Gdansk to the future king

of Poland – Przemysław. In 1308, the city was invaded by the Teutonic Knights and the Polish population was killed. Their rule for the next 158 years had great political, ethnical and material consequences. The German language gained in importance in technological ingenuity that the Order brought with them helped introduce several improvements into the city, such as the Radunia canal delivering water to the windmill wheels. The granting of municipal rights and membership in the Hanseatic League led to the great wealth of Gdansk. Despite its successes, the Teutonic rule caused resentment among the citizens. The first attempt to overthrow the monastic yoke took place in 1410, when after the Polish victory in the battle of Grunwald the citizens paid homage to King Władysław Jagiełło. In 1454, the inhabitants of Gdansk razed the castle, and finally, in 1466, Gdansk returned into Polish hands and the Duke of Prus-

Gdansk. Main Town. Tower of St Mary's Church looming over the houses in Piwna Street (Jopengasse).

Tower clock from 1559 decorating the town hall in the Main Town.

Statue of Neptune in the fountain outside Artus Court.

15th century crane building.

Gdansk. Tops of merchants' houses in Długi Targ St. no. 40, 41 and 42. Number 41 is the famous Golden House with elaborate facade decorations.

sia title remained with the Polish Crown until 1795. The Polish years were the Golden Age for Gdansk. It was the port from which departing ships would feed Europe with Polish and Ukrainian crops. Here the decks were loaded with Latvian and Belarusian pine trees to be shipped to England and the Netherlands as material for masts for their Atlantic-crossing fleets. As was recorded in 1583, 2229 ships left the harbour that year. The wealth of the city had its source both in trade and local production. It was renowned for its breweries, excellent furniture and *Goldwasser*, i.e. vodka with added gold dust. Local jewellery workshops specialising in amber and silver handiwork gained international fame. The goldsmith of Gdansk, Peter van der Rennen, made a sarcophagus for the remains of St Stanisław and presented it to the cathedral. The local production of silver thread supplied all court embroiderers in Europe. The city flourished. The citizens were among the richest and best educated in the whole of *Rzeczypospolita*, which at the time covered an area of one million square kilometres. It was here that the outstanding astronomer, Johannes Hevelius, carried out his research, and the inventor of the thermometer, Gabriel Fahrenheit, was born. The Polish language grew in importance, which manifested itself in the publication of "Polish for foreigners" workbooks. During the "belligerent" 17th century in Poland, Gdansk not only withstood siege on several occasions but also financially assisted the royal treasury with large sums of money. In 1733, the city backed the legally elected king, Stanisław Leszczyński, running against a pro-Russia August III. After Stanisław's defeat it was forced to pay a contribution of one million thalers.

Even though Napoleon considered Gdansk to be "the key to everything" and made it a free city, the period of the partitioning of Poland greatly diminished the city's

◄ *Main Town. Burghers' houses reconstructed after the wartime damage of March 1945.*

Picturesque Mariacka Street with reconstructed perrons, typical of old-time architecture in Gdansk.

importance. Catherine Hübscher, a laundress also known as Madame Sans-Géne, became the Duchess of Gdansk. In the 20th century, Gdansk reappeared on the stage of history, when the Third Reich chose it as the site where it would stage a military provocation. It was here that the first shots of World War II were to be heard on the 1st September 1939 at 4.45am. In March 1945, the merciless offensive by the Red Army left 60 to 90 per cent of all buildings in ruin. Resurrected from the rubble, Gdansk became an important industrial centre of Poland. In 1970, the city witnessed the massacre of workers protesting against the lawlessness of the communist authorities, an event, which ten years later led to the creation of the only legal trade union independent from Moscow within the Eastern Bloc – "Solidarity". Though the mass movement seemed to be stifled, the city remained a centre of pro-independence and anti-communist activism. After the rebirth of the Polish Commonwealth *(Rzeczpospolita Polska)*, Lech Wałęsa, the Gdansk worker, became the country's president.

Among the most precious historical edifices in Gdansk, one should mention the buildings in the Main Town, St Mary's Church *(Kościół Mariacki)*, Wisłoujście Fortress, the Great Arsenal *(Wielka Zbrojownia)*, the City Hall in the Main Town, the Artus Court *(Dwór Artusa)*, the Gdansk Crane *(Żuraw)* and the famous city gates.

Gdansk-Oliwa. Famous Rococo organ screen by J.Wulf in the Romanesque-Gothic cathedral.

Sopot

A walk on the pier is a must for every visitor to Sopot.

Sopot Pier is more than half a kilometre long, out of which 458 metres is over the water of Gdansk Bay.

The Polish Baltic coastline abounds with beautiful sandy beaches. Sopot is the pearl of the coastal spas. Huddled between the industrial ports of Gdansk and Gdynia, it has kept its unique character as a city of leisure. Naturally, the sweet languor applies only to the visitors, and not to the locals, who go out of their way in order to provide board and lodging for the influx of tourists.

For centuries Sopot was just a quiet village. Even its name signifies a murmuring stream. From the 16th century, it acted as a refuge for Gdansk patricians tired of the urban tumult. In 1823, Jan Jerzy Haffner, a former medic in the Napoleonic army, built baths here and propagated a new therapy method, which recommended bathing alternately in cold and heated sea water. In 1901, Sopot was promoted to city status and given its crest: a white seagull

Sopot. Grand Hotel. Ideal place for a Monte Carlo style holiday (if you are away from the Riviera).

Sopot. Square at the entry to the pier.

Sopot. Bohaterów Monte Cassino – the main street.

against a sky-blue background. New appealing facilities were introduced, such as tennis courts and an amphitheatre for 4,000 spectators. After World War I, Sopot found itself within the borders of the Free City of Gdansk. Today, it is a popular centre for cultural life and the amphitheatre annually holds the Sopot International Song Festival. Reaching half a kilometre into the sea, Sopot Pier is one of the major tourist attractions. Even on a nice warm day, it is advisable to bring a pullover for protection against the sea wind. On land, the pier leads into the Bohaterów Monte Cassino Street, the main pedestrian area of Sopot. House number 10 in one of the side streets near the station, Kościuszki Street, is the birthplace of Klaus Kinski, a distinguished German actor (1926-1991).

Gdynia

When Poland's access to Gdansk became limited, a new harbour was built in record speed between the years 1922 and 1926, and around it developed the youngest of Poland's large cities. In 1936, a transatlantic route connected Gdynia with New York. It was serviced by a motorship "Batory", built in Italy and awarded the Blue Riband of the Atlantic. Nowadays, Gdynia has a population of about 250,000 inhabitants and is an important industrial, cultural and academic centre. It has active shipyards, electronic companies and fish processing factories. The Music Theatre of Gdynia is considered to be the best venue of its kind in Poland. Gdynia can also boast several academic institutes: the Gdynia Maritime Academy, the Military Naval Academy, the Sea Fisheries Institute and the Institute of Maritime and Tropical Medicine. Two floating museums are moored in the port. The first is the ORP *Błyskawica*, a ship that took part in the Norwegian campaign of 1940 and later in the Evacuation at Dunkirk. From 1942, it sailed in convoys to Murmansk, shielded the landing troops of the Allied forces in North Africa, and the landing operation in Normandy. The acronym ORP, *Okręt Rzeczpospolitej Polskiej* (Polish Commonwealth's Ship), is the official title for the military units of the Polish Navy. The second floating museum is *Dar Pomorza* (Pomera-

"Dar Pomorza" – antique frigate belonging to the Maritime Academy in Gdynia.

nia's Gift), a beautiful sailing ship, which, as the name betrays, was a gift from the Pomeranian community to the students of the Maritime Academy. It was bought in 1929 and the minister Eugeniusz Kwiatkowski is the ship's "godfather". Konstanty Matyjewicz-Maciejewicz was the first captain under the Polish flag until 1938, and took the frigate on around the world voyage between the years 1934 and 1935.

ORP "Błyskawica" – the ship of WWII, turned into a floating museum.

Hel

Hel. Lighthouse.

To those familiar with the Germanic languages, the name brings to mind "Hell". Indeed, this word is the origin of the place name. It may have even been called "hell" by the Vikings, who recognised the great risk for their ships and sailors created on an unclear day by the narrow stretch of sandy land (in the past, a string of islets) reaching far out to sea. The town situated at the very tip of the peninsula has an interesting museum dedicated to fishing and a research station, dealing with protected mammals in the Baltic Sea: the grey seal and porpoise. Travellers interested in paying a visit to Hel will find a tourist boat from Gdynia to be the easiest route. On a nice day, a trip like this will be unforgettable.

Local Kashubians use the name "Hel" only in reference to the town, whereas the rest of Poland applies it

Cut off from the Baltic by the Hel Peninsula, the waters of Puck Bay are an ideal place for windsurfing.

to the whole peninsula. Many popular holiday resorts can be found here, such as Jurata, Jastarnia, Chałupy and Kuźnica. The fragile natural environment of the peninsula demands sensitive and systematic care from people. Cut off from the open sea, Puck Bay is an ideal place for windsurfing.

◄ Pier in Jurata on the Hel Peninsula.

Dead forest left behind by shifting dunes.

Planting resilient grass types is one of the ways in which the movement of dunes can be prevented.

Remains of dwellings of Słowińcy, descendants of a Slavic tribe of Pomerania.

Łeba's environs. Dunes in the Słowiński National Park.

Słowiński National Park

Situated to the west of Łeba, the Słowiński National Park is the largest wildlife reserve on the Polish coast. It encompasses lakes Gardno, Dołgie Małe, Dołgie and Łebsko (the third largest in Poland), all of which used to be sea bays but were gradually cut off by the accumulation of material on the sand bars (the same phenomenon is observed today near Hel). The second attraction to be found here is a complex of shifting sand dunes, which can measure up to 55 metres in height. The speed with which the dunes travel depends on the wind factor and can reach 20 metres per year. The power of the elements is difficult to harness. During the last several hundred years, the sand buried several villages, including the old Łeba, whose inhabitants had to

Fitting elements of Slovinian cottages.

relocate the town outside the danger zone. The southern Baltic coast is a busy route for spring and autumn bird migrations. The location of the park in this area fosters ornithological study, observation and protection of the bird species occurring here. Within the Park's borders, in Kluki village, there is an open-air museum (*skansen*) featuring the artefacts of the aboriginal Słowińcy tribe, whose Pomeranian dialect survived in the tongues of just a handful of people until the first half of the 20th century. Mt Rowokół (115 m) looms over the eastern shore of the lake Gardno. In the distant past it was a centre of a pagan cult. Remains of bonfires at its top dating back to the 16th-18th centuries prove that it used to serve as a natural beacon.

Kołobrzeg. Gothic cathedral of the Holy Virgin Mary.

Seven candle candelabrum in Kołobrzeg Cathedral.

Kołobrzeg

The small Parsęta river springs from the moraine hills of the central Pomerania and joins the Baltic Sea. Its basin widens during the course of the river and creates several pools which helped foster the creation of a port and a stronghold in the Middle Ages. This is how Kołobrzeg began – one of the major centres of Pomerania. During the reign of Mieszko I and Bolesław Chrobry, Pomeranians accepted their sovereignty. A bishopric was established here in 1000. However, during the lapse back into paganism between 1037 and 1038 Pomerania cut itself off from Poland. The next evangelising mission of 1124 was conducted here by St Otton of Bamberg, after Pomerania had been conquered by Bolesław Krzywousty. Kołobrzeg has never become a large harbour. Its economic existence relied on salt extraction from local brine sources. These sources as well as the stores of mud have created a foundation for the development of a spa.

51

Kołobrzeg. Fortified lighthouse.

Tourist boat in Kołobrzeg harbour.

Kołobrzeg. Crowded beaches in high season. ▶

Therapeutic springs and mud can be also found further inland in the central Pomerania, in Połczyn, for example. Thanks to its favourable climate, medicinal mud and bromic-iodide brine, rich in ions of calcium, iron and magnesium, Kołobrzeg has served as a treatment centre and specialises in rheumatism, diabetes, diseases of the respiratory tract and circulatory system, poisoning and movement disorders. The town has retained some of the interesting historic buildings, such as a Gothic collegiate church that was built before the year 1321, and expanded in the second half of the 14th century to form a five-nave hall. Many elements of its historic interior were salvaged from the fire of 1945, which was started during a fierce battle for the city's independence, and the partial collapse of the church. The reconstruction works of the collegiate were conducted in 1957-58 and 1974-76.

Szczecin. Houses in the Old Town.

Szczecin

Known as the Mother of Pomerania, Szczecin originated from an ancient Slavic settlement at the mouth of the Odra river and in the early 12th century became the capital of the West Pomerania. It changed hands from Polish to Danish to Brandeburg. The Duke Barnim III (1300-1368) re-established it as a ducal metropolis, but from 1630 it was occupied by the Swedes, and then the Prussians from 1720. During World War II, it was demolished because of its importance as an industrial centre and a harbour. About 60 per cent of the residential area, 75 per cent of the industrial infrastructure, and up to 90 per cent of the port was left in ruins. In the spring of 1945, it was occupied by the Red Army, and in July handed over to the Polish administration. It was finally announced part of Poland during the Potsdam Confer-

ence. It is the largest city in the north-west of the country, populated by nearly 420,000 inhabitants. It is a significant trading harbour and a sailing centre. The major historic sites of the city include: the Cathedral of St Jacob the Apostle, the Old Town Hall and the Castle of the Pomeranian Princes. The cathedral was built between the years 1375 and 1387, then converted several times and rebuilt after the ravages of war in 1971-75. Its tower, constructed in 1504, originally measured 119 metres, but today is only half the size. The Town Hall is a reconstruction, which was undertaken after 1945 in an attempt to give it back its 15th century appearance. The same applies to the castle, which was redecorated to resemble its form at the turn of the 16th century. In the beginning of the 20th century, the former military fort, located

◀ *Szczecin. Fragment of the Old Town.*

south-east of the castle, next to the Wały Chrobrego Street, was supplanted by a line of splendid, monumental buildings. The top of the rampart overlooks the panorama of the harbour. South of the city, there stretches a miniature mountain range – a string of moraine hills called the Beech Mountains *(Góry Bukowe)* owing to the beech forests overgrowing it.

Little street near the Castle of the Pomeranian Princes.

Clock decorating one of the castle towers.

Castle of the Pomeranian Princes. ▶

54

One of the monumental buildings in Wały Chrobrego St.

Panorama of Wały Chrobrego boulevard seen from the harbour.

Architectural decoration of the steps in Wały Chrobrego St.

Cathedral of SS Peter and Paul in Ostrów Tumski.

Cathedral of SS Peter and Paul. The Golden Chapel.

Poznan (Poznań)

Cathedral of SS Peter and Paul. Gothic main altar.

Located on the middle Warta, Poznan is the largest city of Wielkopolska. Its history is very closely related to the origins of Polish Christianity. In 968, the first bishopric was founded here. Its priest, Jordan, a missionary bishop, was directly under the authority of the Vatican. This laid the foundations for the hierarchy of the Polish church and established its independence from the bishops of the Holy Roman Empire. During Jordan's times, on an island called Ostrów Tumski cut off from the mainland by the inlets of the Warta river, there existed a stronghold encircled by a massive wall made of earth and wood. At its base, the rampart was ten metres thick and measured over nine metres in height. As a result of archaeological research of the remains, and from the written records describing such constructions, it has been estimated that to build one meter of the wall the builders utilised 4 cubic metres of stone, 42 cubic metres of wood and around 46 cubic metres of earth. The transportation of such amounts of material (as indicated by Tomasz Jurasz)

Houses at the Old Town Square.

required 155 horse-drawn carts that mean four thirty-ton freight cars in today's terms. Despite the mighty fortifications, Poznan was not saved from the siege of a Bohemian prince Bretislav in 1038, after which the town's importance diminished.

The second phase in Poznań's development is related to the trading settlement started on the left bank of the Warta river in 1253. From that point onwards, trade became the major source of the town's wealth, and even more so after 1394. In that year, King Władysław Jagiełło decreed that all traders passing

"Bamberka" – a sculpture at the entrance to the Poznan Town Hall.

through would have to put their goods on sale.

The inherent commercial character of Poznan was again made apparent in the 19th century, when the inhabitants of Wielkopolska successfully managed to build an independent Polish economy under Prussian domination. Beginning with the intensification of farming and the modernisation of crafts, Poznan was to go through a period of industrial boom. It saw the development of food processing and production of farming equipment. One of those factories, belonging to Hipolit Cegielski, has been transformed into a modern manufactur-

Poznan goats lock antlers every hour on the town hall tower.

Frontage of the Raczyński Library.

ing plant, today churning out diesel engines, air compressors, blowing fans, trams, and tools and devices for their maintenance.

After 1919, when Poznan returned to Poland as a result of the Wielkopolska Uprising, it found itself among the leading industrial cities. From 1925, it has been the site of a major International Fair, offering 14 huge air-conditioned trading hall pavilions, with a total exhibition area of 110,000 m² and 32,000 m² of land with full infrastructure for light development.

The city abounds in historic sites. The oldest of them is Poznan Cathedral. Built in the Romanesque style in 1050-75, and then rebuilt in the Gothic style in the 13th century, it occupies the spot where there used to be an even older church demolished by Bretislav. The Golden Chapel holds a sarcophagus containing the bodies of the first historic rulers of Poland: the Duke Mieszko I and his son, King Bolesław Chrobry. The Town Hall in the Old Town Square, built on the foundations belonging to an earlier Gothic structure, is a reminder of the Renaissance glory of the city. It was erected between the years 1550 and 1560 in the North-Italian Renaissance style by Giovanni Battista Quadro. The magnificent interiors of the Town Hall (particularly the hall on the first floor) are accessible to the public during the opening hours of the museum, which is also located here. The most beautiful example of Poznan's Baroque architecture is the former Jesuit parish church, which due to wartime disruption (conflicts with Sweden and Russia) took 75 years to complete (1651-1725). Its interior, which is rather small, gives an impression of unlimited space thanks to the shape of the building and the play of light. The viewing perspective of the visitor changes depending if they are standing or kneeling.

◀ *Poznan Town Hall, one of the most important examples of Polish Renaissance architecture.*

Knights' Castle in Kórnik near Poznań, rebuilt as a neo-Gothic palace.

Kórnik

Kórnik is a small town in the Gniezno Lake District, situated on the stretch of land dividing the lakes Kórnickie and Skrzynki. It is about 20 kilometres south-east of Poznań. In the 15th century it belonged to a wealthy family of the Górka. As time went by, the Kórnik estates changed hands and diminished in size. Kórnik has associations with a few aristocratic clans: the Szołdrski, the Działyński, and the Zamoyski. The last owner of the Kórnik castle, Władysław Zamoyski, bequeathed it to the nation along with the priceless collections of art and the library.

The neo-Gothic castle of Tytus Adam and Jan Kanty Działyński was given its current form in 1843-60. The design for reconstruction work was drafted by the well

Lion guarding entry to the palace in Kórnik.

60

Fragment of the arboretum in Kórnik.

known Berlin architect Friedrich Schinkel in 1835. It was erected with the use of building material taken from the walls of the medieval castle belonging to the Górka family, which had existed there since the end of the 14th century. The building was located on an island surrounded by a moat. Nearby, is a large park and a botanic garden covering the total area of nearly 33.5 hectares. The local arboretum holds the largest collection of trees and shrubs in Poland, representing around three thousand species and variants. It is looked after by the Institute of Dendrology of the Polish Academy of Sciences *(PAN – Polska Akademia Nauk)*. The Academy also manages the castle library. The collection of books, primarily acquired by the Działyński family, contains invaluable manuscripts (including those by Adam Mickiewicz, the most famous Polish Romantic poet) and very rare and old publications, such as the first edition of the astronomical thesis by Nicholas Copernicus *De revolutionibus*. The museum, which is located within the castle, provides access to the residential wing of the building with unique 19th century floors made by the local craftsmen. It also houses the personal effects of Władysław Zamoyski, and collections of archaeological, botanical and ethnographical nature, including Malagasy, Polynesian and Australian displays.

Wisława Szymborska, the poet and winner of the Nobel Prize for Literature in 1996, was born on the other side of the Kórnik Lake, in a place called Bnin. Her father worked as the manager of the Kórnik estates.

View of the palace in Rogalin from the park.

Rogalin

Some 20 kilometres west of Kórnik and south of Poznań, stretches the Wielkopolski National Park. It protects the postglacial terrain formations created by Baltic Glaciation, such as moraine hills, eskers and lakes, as well as the natural environments that developed in that region during the last ten thousand years after the glacier receded.

In the village of Rogalin, located at the entrance to the Wielkopolski National Park, there is yet another family residence, the palace of the Raczyński clan. In its neighbourhood, lies a primeval oak forest, the largest in Poland and one of the largest in Europe, consisting of approximately a thousand ancient trees considered to be organic monuments of nature. The most time-honoured of these can be dated at between six and seven hundred years old. The most famous examples are to be found growing in the park immediately adjacent to the castle. The three trees have been named after the founders of the Slavic states: Lech, Czech and Rus. Their dimensions are indeed very impressive: the diameter of the trunk of Lech (at the height of a man's chest) exceeds 9

Sculpture in the park designed by the royal architect J.C.Kamsetzer.

One of the massive oak trees from the largest cluster of such trees in Poland.

A classicistic court's chapel from 1820.

metres. Rogalin oak trees are strictly protected. Paradoxically, Cerambyx Cerdo L., the most harmful oak tree pest, is a local entomological curiosity and also falls under strict environmental protection.

A late Baroque palace was built in Rogalin in 1770. Soon after, between the years 1782 and 1788, it was rebuilt with the addition of Rococo features by the royal architects Dominik Merlini and Jan Christian Kamsetzer. Romantic neo-Gothic elements were introduced to the interior in the middle of the 19th century. The exhibition space located in the palace is affiliated to the National Museum in Poznań, and presents interiors in various artistic styles along with the furniture, porcelain, fabrics and other fittings characteristic of the epoch. The collection of paintings to be found here, was put together thanks to the efforts of Edward Raczyński, and encompasses French and German Romantic art, French Impressionism and the leading Polish painters of the 19th and 20th century: Jan Matejko, Stanisław Wyspiański, Olga Boznańska, Jacek Malczewski, Leon Wyczółkowski and Julian Fałat.

Gniezno

Gniezno is closely linked to the beginnings of Polish statehood. The name of the city has its origins in the word meaning "a nest" *(gniazdo)*. It relates to the story of a white eagle's nest that was found on a big oak tree by Lech, the mythical chief of the Polanie tribe. However, regardless of what the legends say, it has been established that Gniezno existed as a permanent human settlement already at the turn of the 6th century. In the 8th century, upon Mt Lech, there developed a fortified settlement consisting of a stronghold and adjacent dwellings. In the 10th century, the town was elevated in status from being a capital of the tribal dukedom to the capital of Poland, whose ruler, Mieszko I, was baptised here in 966. From the year 1000, Gniezno served as the seat of the archbishop, who initially supervised three dioceses: Kołobrzeg, Wroclaw and Cracow. This came about as a result of the decisions taken during the Gniezno Convention in 1000, when the emperor Otto III came to visit Bolesław Chrobry at the burial place of St Adalbert. After the Bohemian invasion of 1038, Gniezno lost its importance as the leading fortress in the country, but Gniezno Cathedral continued to serve as the coronation site of Polish kings until 1300. From 1419, the title of the Archbishop of Gniezno would be coupled with the title of the Primate of Poland. It was an exceptionally significant role, as in the case of an interregnum, the Primate would serve as the head of state. The Romanesque Archbishop's Cathedral (consecrated in 1064) occupied the site where there used to stand the oldest church in Poland. Regrettably, it was razed during the

View of the cathedral.

Cathedral. Baroque silver sarcophagus holding the relics of St Adalbert.

Priceless masterpiece of Romanesque art, Drzwi Gnieźnieńskie, bronze doors with scenes of the life of St Adalbert.

Gniezno Cathedral. Epitaph of Primate of Poland, cardinal Michał Radziejowski, Gniezno archbishop.

Gniezno Cathedral. Late Gothic tomb of cardinal Zbigniew Oleśnicki made by Veit Stoss.

invasion of the Teutonic Knights in 1331, and replaced by a Gothic church built between 1342 and 1400, which we can see today. Rebuilt in the 17th and 18th century, first in the Baroque and later in a fusion of the Baroque and Classicist style, it was given back its Gothic appearance, during reconstruction works undertaken in the post-war period. Nowadays, it is the major historic site of the city. The most valuable item in the church is a pair of Romanesque doors cast in bronze around the year 1170. They depict scenes from the life of St Adalbert, the patron of Poland and a martyr, whose remains are kept in the cathedral. The relics are contained in a silver coffin made in 1662 by the Gdansk goldsmith Peter van der Rennen, which is now located on the main altar. Another precious element in the interior of the cathedral is the tomb of the archbishop Zbigniew Oleśnicki, dating back to the year 1495, and engraved by Veit Stoss – the greatest medieval sculptor in Central Europe.

During recent times, the status of the city has been retained through the office of the archbishop, but otherwise, Poznan and Kalisz, two major cities of Wielkopolska have outranked Gniezno. During the period of Poland's partition, the city was an important centre of Polish patriotic activism. After it was re-incorporated into Poland, the first people's university was set up here in 1921. Contemporary Gniezno has over 70,000 inhabitants and is an industrial centre. Other historic sites apart from the aforementioned cathedral include the Romanesque Church of St George, rebuilt in the Baroque style in the 17th century, two Gothic turned Baroque temples known as the Holy Trinity and St Laurence, and the Baroque Church of SS Peter and Paul.

Biskupin. Reconstructed street of a wooden town from the Lusatian period. ▶

Biskupin. Panorama of the stronghold.

Biskupin

Language can store ancient knowledge about things lost in time without the speaker being aware of its significance. No one ever suspected the origins of the name *Na grodzichach* used in reference to the peninsula on the Biskupin Lake. In 1933, remains of a two and a half thousand years old stronghold were discovered here. A teacher in the region, Walenty Szwajcer, found out that dried up wooden beams unearthed from beneath a layer of turf covering the peninsula were being used as fuel by local people. He instantly notified the archaeologists. This is how Biskupin, a fortified settlement dating back to the Bronze and the Iron Age, came to be excavated. It was built from oak and pine wood, and inhabited by the representatives of the Lusatian culture. Calling it a town would not be an exaggeration. In its heyday, Biskupin had a population of 1200 inhabitants. Archaeological research conducted by two professors Józef Kostrzewski and Zdzisław Rajewski revealed enough details to allow for a partial reconstruction of the settlement. This included the dwellings sized 8 by 10 metres, wooden paved streets and ramparts constructed on a wooden framework. The Biskupin complex features a museum, an archaeological reserve and an open-air reconstruction of buildings in their authentic sizes. It is visited annually by 150,000 tourists. In the second half of September, it holds a festival dedicated to archaeology.

Biskupin. Gate to the stronghold, recreated on the basis of archaeological research.

Licheń. The old church.

Licheń

Located some ten kilometres from Konin, Licheń is the second most frequented pilgrimage site in Poland and a centre relating to the cult of the Virgin Mary. The massive church erected in this little town towards the end of the 20th century is the largest place of worship in the whole country. The funding for its construction was amassed thanks to the generosity of the pilgrims visiting Licheń. The icon of the Holy Mary of Licheń reputedly has miraculous powers, and it is said to have brought about salvation from the plague. The story of the icon relates to the vision experienced by a Napoleonic soldier, Tomasz Kłossowski, during the Battle of the Nations in Leipzig in 1813. He spent years searching for the miraculous image that was instilled in his mind. He found it in 1836 in Lgota and trans-

Licheń. Picture representing the scene of the sighting of the Virgin Mary.

ferred it to Licheń, where he mounted it on a robust pine tree. Accounts of visions of St Mary were recorded here in 1850, when a shepherd Mikołaj Sikatka heard a call to convert to prayer and give up alcohol as well as being warned against a brooding plague. The cholera epidemics broke out nearly two years later. The pilgrimage movement exploded in 1852, when 80,000 people attended the ceremony of the relocation of the painting to the local church. The sanctuary is famous for its powers to convert people and liberate them from addictions, alcoholism in particular. The visiting pilgrims hoping to change their lives can rely not only on religious ministrations, but can also receive secular advice in the counselling centres adjacent to the church.

Licheń. The new church.

Lodz. Piotrkowska Street, the main shopping street of the city.

Lodz (Łódź)

The history of Lodz, the second largest city in Poland, is a textbook example of a career of a 19th century town, which at an auspicious time focused on the development of industry and a technological revolution. Designated as an industrial settlement in 1821, it started out as an insignificant town of 200 inhabitants. Prussian records from 1796-98 mention 180 Christians and 11 Jews occupying a total of 33 houses. The construction of dwellings for factory workers caused an increase of population to 799 in 1823, and to 4273 five years later. From 1815 the city was under the authority of the autonomous Kingdom of Poland, which supported its industrial growth. In 1839, Ludwik Geyer's factory led the way in putting to use the first steam engine in the city. From that moment onwards, the capitalist industrial revolution turned Lodz into a "promised land". Entrepreneurial spirit and good luck in business combined with organisational talent, hard work and the determination to succeed came to fruition in the form of multimillion fortunes. The estate owned by Karol Scheibler, who arrived in Lodz in 1854 with just hand luggage and a modest sum of money to start a workshop, skyrocketed in 1881 to the net worth of 14 million roubles. The city became a multinational and multicultural conglomerate, inhabited by Poles, Ger-

Piotrkowska Street. Statue of the poet Julian Tuwim with the palace of the Heinzl family in the background (today the Town Hall).

◀ *Licheń. The interior of the main nave in the new church.*

71

Lodz. Villa of Edward and Matylda Herbst. A wedding gift from Matylda's father, Karol Scheibler.

Lodz. Factory in Księży Młyn.
The cotton empire of Karol Scheibler.

mans, Jews, Russians and representatives of several other nationalities. Today, Lodz boasts the most impressive complex of historic 19th century industrial architecture in Poland. It also has the longest shopping street in Europe, the Piotrkowska, which runs for four kilometres, and one of the first museums dedicated to avant-garde art in the world – the Museum of Art, set up in 1931. Lodz can be proud of the School of Cinema, Television and Theatre, which produced such graduates as Krzysztof Kieślowski and Andrzej Wajda; and also the Polish Language Study Center for Foreigners – an institution which has taught Polish to over 15,000 visitors from abroad. As part of its tragic heritage, Lodz is also the location of the largest Jewish cemetery in Europe – the burial place of about 200,000 people.

Lodz. Israel K. Poznański's Palace, now the Museum of Lodz History.

Lodz-Doły. The tomb of the Poznański family in the largest Jewish cemetery in Europe.

French Renaissance castle.

Gołuchów

Gołuchów Castle brings to mind the French residences in the Loire Valley. This is not surprising, as its current appearance is a result of the French neo-Renaissance fashion, which held sway in the whole of Europe in the 1870s and 1890s.

From the 15th century there existed a medieval castle belonging to the Leszczyński family, (we could trace one more French connection here, as Maria the daughter of Stanisław Leszczyński, the king of Poland and a Lotharingian prince, married Louis XV, the King of France). In the second half of the 19th century, Gołuchów estates became the property of the Działyński family. Izabela Działyńska née Czartoryska commissioned two architects Zygmunt Gorgolewski and Maurycy August Ouradou to undertake the reconstruction of the castle. The works took place between the years 1872 and 1885. The castle became a three-wing building arranged on an irregular plan with an arcade courtyard and five turrets. Authentic 16th century window masonry (frames and sculptures) was imported from Italy and France. The neighbouring buildings were given a French aspect, and a landscape park, designed personally by the castle owners Izabela and Jan Działyński, was laid out around the residence.

Before 1939 the castle housed a museum, which was devastated during the Nazi occupation. After World War II, the interiors of the castle were restored and today they hold a branch of the National Museum of Poznań.

Fragment of the castle park with the view of the outbuilding.

74

Town Hall in the Main Town Square.

Kalisz

Even though the interpretation of the text from the 2nd century AD written by an Alexandrian geographer Claudius Ptolemy poses some difficulty, we could safely say that his mention of Kalisia in the year 150 refers to the Polish Kalisz. It existed then as a trading post on the Amber Road on the river Prosna, and its function was to help maintain the commercial exchange between the Roman Empire and the Baltic coast. After this little reference, there is nearly a one thousand year gap in the

Kalisz. Main altar in St Nicholas Church.

history of the town. The next mention of Kalisz comes from the year 1106 and describes a dispute over a stronghold between Bolesław Krzywousty and his brother Zbigniew. A few clerical buildings in Kalisz have medieval origins. This includes the Church of St

Nicholas, the Franciscan Monastery with the Church of St Stanisław, as well as the wooden Church of St Adalbert in Zawodzie. Even though the current day parish church was built in 1798, it is quite certain that the first parish of the settlement was established in the 11th century. During the restoration works, it was discovered that the flat block of sandstone constituting the doorstep to the church was in fact the tombstone of Mieszko the Elder, the Duke of Wielkopolska and a senior ruler of Poland, who was buried in Kalisz in 1202. The majority of the historic heritage of the city was wiped out during the Prussian bombing and arson attacks of August 1914. The number of inhabitants dropped dramatically at the time from 70,000 to 5,000.

Wroclaw. Town Hall.

Wroclaw (Wrocław)

Wroclaw. Clock on the Town Hall's facade.

Wroclaw, the capital city of the Lower Silesia, is the largest industrial, academic and cultural centre in south-west Poland. The turbulent and complicated history of the place is considered to be representative of the development of a Central European city. Wroclaw bishopric was established in 1000 and reported directly to the Polish metropolis of Gniezno. This proves that by that time Wroclaw had already become an important city. Archaeological research confirms the existence of a Neolithic settlement in the period 2500-1700 B.C. and during the Lusatian age (1300-400 B.C.). The discovery of Roman coins suggests that it was situated on the Amber Road. In the early Middle Ages, there were two strongholds belonging to the Ślężanie tribe, (which betrays the origins of the name of the whole Silesian region – *Śląsk*). These guarded the crossing on the river Odra. Before 966, Silesia belonged to Bohemia and was annexed to Poland as a dowry of the Czech princess Dubravka, who married Mieszko I. In 1000, the original town of Wroclaw consisted of a system of strongholds and fortified trading settlements. Formally, Wroclaw was granted the municipal charter around the year 1241. During that time, Poland was in a state of fragmentation as a consequence of Bolesław Krzywousty's idea to divide the country among his heirs. Therefore, Silesia was in the hands of the Silesian Piast rulers – the descendants of Władysław II Wygnaniec. Although they retained their Polish ducal titles, the region was practically outside Polish borders. By 1675 all lines of the Piast dynasty died out in Silesia, and their districts were taken over by Czech rulers. Some Silesian dukes accepted the suzerainty of Bohemia, others continued to be Polish allies. The Wroclaw Duchy was annexed to Bohemia in 1335. However, due to the close proximity, the city maintained its relations with

Wroclaw. Restored houses in the Main Town Square with St Elisabeth's Church in the background.

Wroclaw. Grunwald Bridge.

Poland. In 1471, Władysław Jagiellończyk, the son of the Polish King Kazimierz Jagiellończyk, ascended the Bohemian throne, and as a result Wroclaw and Silesia were re-incorporated into Poland. The House of Jagiellon now controlled Polish, Ukrainian, Belarusian, Lithuanian, Latvian, and from 1490 also Hungarian and Slovakian territories. The vast expanse of the powerful Lithuanian-Polish dynasty lasted until 1526, when the southern dependencies, including Bohemia and Silesia, were taken over by the House of Habsburg. In 1741, Wroclaw was invaded by the Prussians. During the 19th century, the city rose to be among the leading industrial

Wroclaw. Stained-glass window over the main altar in the cathedral.

Wroclaw. Cathedral's main nave.

Wroclaw. Cathedral's main nave.

centres of Germany. In 1936, several sport competitions of the XI Olympic Games in Berlin hosted by Hitler were held in Wroclaw. With the Red Army at the gates in winter 1945, the decision was made to evacuate the civilians and turn the city into a fortress. It withstood the siege even longer than Berlin, which, as a consequence, led to the annihilation of about 70 per cent of the city. Wroclaw returned to Poland as one of the most tragically scarred places in the world. The population count dropped from a million to nearly zero, as the surviving Germans were exiled under the Yalta agreement. Their place was taken by Poles, who were transferred here from west Ukrainian cities, and predominantly from Lvov (as stipulated under Yalta Conference agreements).

Today's Wroclaw has a population of about 620,000 inhabitants. The historic centre of the city is situated on the archipelagos of river islands, and the residential areas lie in the flat and wide valley of the river Odra. Many arms of the river and a few tributaries create a water grid, which, along with the Gothic church towers, forms the very picturesque panorama that made the city famous. However, the river can also be a source of danger. In July 1997, heavy rains in the Sudetes Mountains resulted in a rapid rise of the water level in several Silesian rivers. The surge of water in the Odra hit Opole and spilled into the Wroclaw region. Historic sites, miraculously saved from the war and from the plundering which followed it, as well as those that had been restored

Wroclaw. Former Jesuit Church of St Matthias, paintings by Johann M. Rottmayer from 1704-06.

Church of St Matthias. Main altar with the painting depicting the scene of Presenting Jesus in the Temple.

with great care, were once more in jeopardy. The heroic response from the city's residents helped to salvage these sites. They spent several days piling up sand bags and guarding the provisional ramparts around the most precious historic areas, regardless of the fact that the river could have been flooding their own homes in the newer residential districts. The city's authorities were so inspired by this collective effort that they submitted their application for Wroclaw to host the EXPO exhibition. They were now convinced that the city could overcome all difficulties.

Visitors coming to Wroclaw are advised to see the architectural complex of Ostrów Tumski with its looming Cathedral of St John the Baptist, which was built in several stages from 1244. It is worthwhile visiting the Romanesque Church of St Idzi, the Gothic churches of St Martin, the Holy Cross and the SS Peter and Paul. Also, one should not miss the monastery complex on the

Piasek Island and the historic buildings of the Old Town, mainly the Town Hall with its historical exhibition and interesting cellars, as well as the former Jesuit buildings of the Wroclaw University with the fairy-tale like Baroque aula.

One of the biggest attractions of the city is the Racławice Panorama (*Panorama Racławicka*), which has been transported here from Lvov. It is a painting shaped like a hyperboloid of revolution, which represents the victorious battle of Tadeusz Kościuszko at Racławice in 1794. The creators of the panoramic painting, Jan Styka and Wojciech Kossak, worked with seven other artists. The canvas is 15 metres high and 120 metres long. It was painted in 1893-94 and displayed in Lvov until 1944. It returned to Poland as part of the post-war vindications and after many years of effort, it was finally made accessible to the public in 1985.

It is also recommended to include in the city's sightseeing programme a river boat trip on the Odra.

Legnica. Church of SS Peter and Paul.

Legnica

Polish history textbooks will often contain a reproduction of an image representing the Tartar siege of Legnica Castle in 1241, taken from a 14th century series of miniatures entitled "The Legend of St Jadwiga". Painted some 150 years after the event, the image depicts the castle as having high towers and crenellated walls. The author exaggerated the level of technological advancement in the architecture of the 13th century Legnica, but only slightly. Legnica was indeed the first stronghold in Poland to include stone towers (called the towers of last resort), which were designed exclusively for defensive purposes and complemented the system of wood-and-earth fortifications. Moreover, even before the Tartar invasion, works were undertaken to replace the rampart with a proper wall. The Duke of Silesia, Henryk Pobożny, fell during the battle of Legnica, but his son, Bolesław Rogatka, started the Piast dynasty of the Legnica-Brzesk province, which held onto the local throne until 1675. The Legnica-Brzesk Duchy separated itself from Silesia in 1248 and Legnica functioned as the cap-ital of the Duchy for 427 years. Out of all Polish cities, only Kraków can boast a longer period of service as a capital, unless we are to take into account the time when Warsaw was the capital of the Mazovian Duchy. Several historic sites of the glorious days have survived in Legnica until today, such as the fragments of the 14th century Gothic city walls, including the gates: Chojnowska and Głogowska. As regards the castle, only the towers and the outer walls betray the original Gothic design. The whole structure was thoroughly rebuilt in the 16th century to become a Renaissance residence. The Gothic style is represented here by the Church of SS Peter and Paul, a bricked structure with stone decorations, built in four stages between the years 1329 and 1390. Another example of Gothic architecture is the Church of the Holy Virgin Mary, built in brick and stone before 1386, extended in the 15th century and rebuilt and refurbished in 1824-25 in cooperation with Karl Friedrich Schinkel. The Baroque Mausoleum of the Piast dynasty, which used to be a Gothic Presbytery, is now

Beautiful Madonna, a sculpture in Legnica Cathedral.

The Gothic towers retained their character despite many transformations of the ducal castle.

Legnica. Art Nouveau houses from the turn of the 19th century.

New Town Hall built in a historical style between 1902-05.

joined with the Church of St John the Baptist, built in the late Baroque style. It is adorned with sculptures of Matthias Rauchmiller. Lubiąż Abbotts' Castle, which currently houses the Museum of Copper, is also Baroque in design. The first museum in Legnica was founded in 1879, but both the building and the collection were annihilated in the military offensive of 1945. Several years after the war, copper-rich deposits were discovered in the vicinity of Legnica. They have become the foundation for the development of the Legnica industrial district, which today belongs to the world's largest centres for copper production and is also a big supplier of silver. The exhibition in the museum presents various aspects of the use of copper and its alloys: the geological, technological, historic and cultural aspects. The collection consists of copper-rich minerals, tools, old weapons, household equipment and artistic copperware. Also to be found here is a collection of time pieces portraying the history and the culture of the region from the oldest periods to contemporary times.

Śnieżka, the highest peak of the Karkonosze and the Sudetes Mountains (1602 m).

The Karkonosze Mountains

On a nice day, the mountain chain of the Sudetes is clearly visible from the southern rim of the Silesian Lowland, rising about 1000 metres above the plains. It is an old range of mountains, rugged and lifted for the second time during the Alpine orogenesis. The whole chain culminates with the ridgeline of the Karkonosze Mountains, situated on the Polish-Czech border, with its highest peak Śnieżka (1602 m). These exceptionally picturesque mountains have long been an area of tourist importance. The beginnings of tourism have their roots in the once intensive pilgrimage movement in the Sudetes region. The whole Sudetes range is an area rich in natural resources and mineral waters, whereas the Karkonosze also used to be exploited for gold and are known for glass manufacturing industry. The most prominent slopes of the Karkonosze are protected and included in the Karkonosze National Park. The park covers an area of 5,575 hectares, of which 30 per cent belongs to the strict reserve. The park is visited yearly by two to three million tourists, which poses a demanding task for the park's management to try and reconcile the protection of the natural beauty of the mountains with the people's need to admire them. Within the park boundaries, visitors are allowed to use only the designated footpaths, of which there are 200 kilometres in total. During winter, Karkonosze turns into skier territory with a system of designated pistes, while the footpaths become less accessible due to the threat of avalanches. In the 1970s and 1980s, Karkonosze and the neighbouring mountain ranges were often victims of acid rains created by the surrounding industrial centres in the Czech Republic, Germany and Poland. This caused the extermination of huge man-planted spruce forests. Today, we can observe how nature in the affected regions has managed to recreate the natural plant life and complete biocenoses (with just a little help of man). Tourist activity is supported by two major urban centres of the area, Szklarska Poręba and Karpacz, little towns characterised by Alpine style architecture. Tourist chalets tucked away in the mountains also play an important role.

Centre of Karpacz. ▶

Karpacz Górny. The Wang Chapel transported from Norway and built from Vikings' boats.

Książ Castle.

Książ

Książ Castle. Coat of arms wall at Black Courtyard (Czarny Dziedziniec).

Silesia is famous for its many defensive structures of historic value, out of which the most renowned are the mountain fortresses protecting the medieval trading routes between Poland and Bohemia and from Western Europe to Ruthenia. Built by kings, princes, bishops, and even by wealthy knights, the castles were later either turned into residences of modern age Silesian families or fell into ruin. One of the castles, whose story could represent the fate of many Silesian forts, is Książ near Wałbrzych. It lies within the administrative borders of Wałbrzych on an elevation of over 400 m and is cut off by a deep gorge of the Pełcznica river. It is the third largest castle in Poland. The fortress was built towards the end of the 13th century at the order of the Duke Bolko I of the Świdnica-Jawor province, to defend the border of the duchy. After Silesia was taken over by Bohemian kings, the castle found itself deep within the country and its protective function lost its importance. The king's administrators no longer paid much attention to the building. It fell into the hands of the knights of the road, who plagued the Silesian trading routes in the 15th century. In 1497, Władysław Jagiellończyk sold it for 600,000 Bohemian groschen to the Schellnberg family. After several other transactions, Książ came into the possession of the Hochberg family, who owned it until 1941. The castle acquired its current shape thanks to two reconstructions conducted in 1548-1555 and 1648-1655, and two extension projects in 1670-1724 and 1909-1923. The final effect is very harmonious despite the complexity of the design, which combines the Gothic base with elements of Renaissance, Baroque and historical stylisation. The interiors consist of 400 rooms, which used to be heated by 200 fireplaces. Individual rooms are still decorated with original, antique inlaid and encrusted panelling, marble and sandstone masonry, stuccowork and polychromies on the walls and the ceilings, upholstery, sculptures and artistic ironwork.

The last owner of Książ to be related to the Hochberg family was the Duchess Maria Teresa Olivia Cornwallis-

◀ *Książ Castle. St George's Tower in the western wing of the castle.*

Książ. Artistic iron cast gate at the entrance near the stud farm.

Książ. Fountain at the castle patio.

Książ. Flora's patio at the foot of the castle, next to the Gunpowder Tower.

Książ. Baroque, eastern facade of the castle.

West, also known as Daisy, the wife of Hans Heinrich XV. After divorce, she became the sole proprietor of the castle and survived the Nazi confiscation of the estate, which was an act of punishment for her sons fighting against Hitler. After 1941, the Germans attempted to transform the castle into an official residence of Hitler.

The work was particularly intensive in the underground vaults, where the Nazis wanted to create a system of bunkers. The rumours say that there are cellars yet to be discovered. Allegedly, they would have been used to store the gold plundered and carted away from Wroclaw in the winter of 1945, or maybe even the Amber Chamber (a set of lavishly gilded panels) stolen from the Tsarskoe Selo, the summer residence of the Russian tsars, during the Leningrad blockade. Nowadays, the 900 metres of tunnels winding beneath the castle are occu-

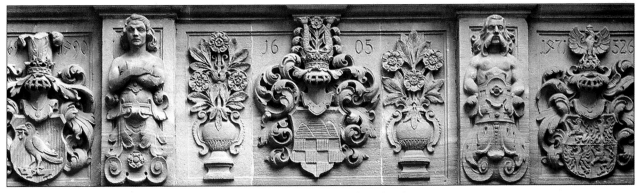

Książ. Frieze on the coat of arms wall with the escutcheon of the von Hochberg family.

Książ Castle. Two-tier ballroom.

pied by the Lower Silesian Geophysical Observatory of the Polish Academy of Sciences, which conducts research on the drifting movement of the earth's crust, measuring the gravitational field of the Earth, as well as recording distant and near seismic disturbances. In the neighbourhood of the castle, there is a stud farm with antique stables, a carriage house and beautiful indoors-riding stables. The farm hosts international carriage driving and horse taming competitions, as well as horse auctions.

Książ Castle. Castle chamber.

Książ. Stud farm buildings.

Kłodzko. Panorama of the town overlooking from the fortress.

Kłodzko

Kłodzko, the main city of the Kłodzko Basin (*Kotlina Kłodzka*) is located in the eastern Sudetes and surrounded by a mountain chain. It was incorporated into Poland only in 1945. Previously, it remained part of the Bohemian Sudetes until 1742, when it was separated from the Habsburg territory by the Prussians. That would explain why the local architecture brings to mind the scenery of the Czech Republic, whose cultural influence was always present here. Even the pearl of medieval engineering, the Charles Bridge in Prague, has its smaller replica in Kłodzko. The castle is situated on the hill overlooking the city. It was expanded after 1622, and in the 18th century an attempt was made to transform it into a modern day citadel. The works commissioned by the Habsburg dynasty were interrupted by the Prussian invasion in 1742. After the Silesian wars, which solidified the annexation of Kłodzko to Prussia, a huge fortress and one of the most interesting buildings of the epoch was erected here. The first stage of work was conducted according to the design of an accomplished Prussian fortifications specialist Gerhard Cornelius Wallrave. The fortress was conquered by the Austrians in 1760 during the Seven Years' War. After the war (1763), the Prussians returned to Kłodzko and undertook work to improve the defensive aspect of the fort. The medieval castle was dismantled and in its place appeared a new structure with a multilateral courtyard, a cylindrical observation tower, a chain of bastions and a three-level basement. Other works conducted at the time gave the whole complex its final form, which has changed very little since. The fortress lost its military importance after the Napoleonic Wars and was turned into a prison. The Prussians kept here Polish patriots, and the Nazis used it to detain Communists. During World War II, it served as a labour camp with a manufacturing department of transmitters and receivers for V1 and V2 rackets. Today, the fortress houses a museum. Some parts of the underground passages are inaccessible, and some were probably cut off or concealed towards the end of the war. This resulted in a proliferation of stories of hidden treasures in Silesia.

89

Kłodzko. Medieval bridge with Baroque sculptures on the Młynówka river.

Kłodzko Fortress.

Duszniki Zdrój. Pump-room of mineral healing waters.

Duszniki Zdrój. Interior of the pump-room.

Kudowa Zdrój. Cardiological sanatorium "Zameczek".

Kudowa Zdrój. Zdrojowy Park and sanatorium "Polonia".

Health Resorts of the Kłodzko Basin

The true treasure of this land, and what is more, accessible to everyone, are the mineral waters of the local health resorts. Kudowa, Polanica, Duszniki, Długopole, Lądek are place names, which are always compounded with the word *Zdrój* – a health spa. Towns situated in the western and southern part of the Basin are famous for the curative waters while Lądek Zdrój specialises in thermal, radon, fluoride and sulphide water therapies. Patients undergoing treatment in this region of Poland have the opportunity to enjoy many attractions, ranging from mountain hikes to classical music concerts. The chains of mountains surrounding the Kłodzko Basin are varied from the geological and morphological point of view. The eastern ranges: Góry Złote, Góry Bialskie and Masyw Śnieżnika would appeal to the enthusiasts of intensive tourism involving long marches and climbs, which demand good physical fitness. The highlight of the Bialskie Mountains is the Niedźwiedzia Cave (literally, the Bear's Cave) in Kletno. The western rim is made up of the Stołowe Mountains, which draw tourists

Spa pavilion.

to their fairy-tale like rocky labyrinths of Wielki Szczeliniec and Błędne Skały. The town situated at the foot of those mountains, Dusznik, used to be frequented by Fryderyk Chopin for medical purposes. This is commemorated nowadays by a summer festival of music. The Orlickie Mountains are very attractive in wintertime. A local curiosity is the Box of Matches Museum situated next to the Matches Manufacturing Plant in Bystrzyca Kłodzka, the only one of its kind in Poland and the Museum of Papermaking in Duszniki.

Viewpoint from a precipice in the Stołowe Mountains.

Opole. Historic house in the Town Square.

Opole

The word *opole* stands for a medieval type of territorial community, in which free land owners would share among themselves a part of the estate. This form of collective farming was popular among Western Slavs on the territory of today's Mecklemburg, Lusatia and Poland. However, from the economic point of view it proved to be less efficient than individual farming and gradually disappeared in the 13th and 14th century. What remained are the place names, the most famous of which refers to the town on the river Odra, situated in the eastern part of the Silesian Lowland. In the early history of Poland, Opole was among the more important urban settlements. It received municipal rights even before 1217. During the period of Poland's fragmentation Opole served as a capital of a duchy. The line of Opole Piast dynasty died out in 1532 with the last representative Jan II Dobry, whose tomb, situated in the local cathedral, is held in great veneration among the city's inhabitants. He was probably the last non-German speaking Silesian duke. Between the years 1645 and 1666, Opole, along with the whole province, was in the hands of the Polish kings of the Vasa dynasty, but fell under Prussian domination after the Silesian wars of the 18th century. Despite the long period of detachment from Poland, in the 19th century Opole was a strong centre of Polish political, cultural and economic organisations. Towards the end of the 20th century, fifty years

Opole. The Amphitheatre in Opole where the National Festival of Polish. Songs is held annually.

Opole. Gothic interior of the Finding of the Holy Cross Cathedral.

after border changes agreed at Yalta, the Opole province became in turn a seat of German cultural life within Poland. In terms of culture, Opole is most often associated with the Festival of Polish Song with forty years of tradition. It is held in a beautiful amphitheatre at the foot of a Gothic tower and attracts professional performers of popular music and new aspiring pop-idols. The title "Opole, Capital of Polish Song" is used in the heading on the official website of the city (www.opole.pl). Slightly less present in the media, but much appreciated by the more sophisticated audience, is the stage life of Opole. The city of 130,000 inhabitants has several theatres, and for the last thirty years it has held the festival: Opole Theatrical Confrontations (*Opolskie Konfrontacje Teatralne*). Between 1959 and 1964, there existed here *Teatr 13 Rzędów*, the Theater of Thirteen Rows, which was run by Jerzy Grotowski (1932-1999), and later evolved into the Laboratory Theatre and moved to Wroclaw. Both the stage and the director are considered to be among the five most significant phenomena of the avant-garde movement in 20th century performing arts. Opole also has a young but dynamically growing university, and four museums: the Museum of Opole Silesia, the Central Museum of Prisoners of War, the Diocesan Museum and the Opole Village Museum.

The city's major historic sites are the Gothic and Baroque churches, including the aforementioned Cathedral of the Finding of the Holy Cross, the remnants of medieval fortifications: city walls and the castle, as well as the Baroque architecture in the neighbourhood of the Town Square.

▼ *Opole. Buildings close to the river banks of the Odra give the impression of a town built on water.*

Wadowice

Pope John Paul II

In the spring of 2005, this small town, with a population of just above 20,000, was the most televised town of this size in all world-broadcasting stations. The square in front of the Church of Devotion of Holy Virgin Mary was filled with 30,000 burning candles. The Pope John Paul II died on the 2nd of April. He was born here under the name Karol Wojtyła on 18th May 1920 in house number two near the Town Square. Wadowice is the place of the Pope's childhood and school days. He graduated from the local gymnasium in May 1938. He nurtured his spiritual life in the Sodality of the Blessed Virgin Mary affiliated to the school, and developed his acting skills in the school theatre group: his debut of 1935 was the role of Haemon in Sophocles *Antigone*. As Pope, he visited his home town on three occasions: 7th June 1979, 14th August 1991 and 16th June 1999. The homily read out during his last visit contained the Pope's personal recollections from the days of his youth. The full text can be found online on the website www.wadowice.pl. The town has taken great care of all memorabilia related to this great man for the Polish nation. His family home today houses a museum.

Family home of Karol Wojtyła.

Wadowice. Memorial plaque on Karol Wojtyła's home.

Wadowice. Church square.

Hitler's concentration camp Auschwitz-Birkenau.

Memorial to the victims of Auschwitz-Birkenau.

Auschwitz

The Polish name of the town is not as recognised (maybe fortunately) as the German version – Auschwitz. The terrains of Hitler's concentration camps Auschwitz-Birkenau have been included in the UN World Heritage Sites, though they most certainly represent the world heritage of shame and barbarity. They constitute physical proof of Nazi crimes committed against the Jews (it is estimated, that 90 per cent of victims were Jewish) and other persons of the countries occupied by the Third Reich, that is Austria, the Czech Republic, Poland, Denmark, Norway, Holland, Belgium, Luxemburg, France, Yugoslavia, Greece, Lithuania, Latvia, Estonia, Soviet Union and Italy, as well as Germany, Romania, Hungary, Slovakia, Spain, Switzerland, Turkey, Great Britain and the United States.

The negation of facts related to the existence of these sites is described by the term Oświęcim Denial (*kłamstwo oświęcimskie*) and is criminalised in many countries, including Poland. Therefore, all data involving the number of murdered victims can only be quoted after the official publications of unquestionable academic value. The Auschwitz-Birkenau camp was created at the order of Heinrich Himmler dated April 1940. The first prisoners were Poles brought here from overcrowded German prisons in June that year. After the extension works of 1941, the camp became a "death factory", to which Jews were transported from all over Europe. The majority of them would be murdered in gas chambers directly after arrival and their bodies would be burned in crematories or forwarded for industrial processing. The victims' hair was used to produce mattresses, and human fat was used to produce soap. Other causes of death in the camp were: hunger, exhaustion from slave labour, beating, torture, executions (including starvation) and medical experiments conducted on the prisoners. Initially, all criminal activity was carefully documented. The SS managed to destroy part of the existing records, but the rest was intercepted by the Red Army, who liberated the camp on 27th January 1945. After the collapse of Communism in 1989, Polish-Israeli relations were revived. The idea to counter crime and death with memory and life was realised through the organisation of the March of the Living, which is held here each spring with the participation of the ex-prisoners, as well as young people from Israel and Poland.

Cracow (Kraków)

The existence of a permanent human settlement within the borders of today's Cracow is estimated to be approximately 5 thousand years old. Traces of the oldest dwelling place are to be found in Wawel – the hill, where there used to exist a stronghold later superseded by the royal castle. The formation of the town itself began in the 8th century, during the rule of the Vistulanians tribe, whose capital must have been Wawel. In the 9th and 10th century, the town was under the sway of the Great Moravian Empire, and later became part of Bohemia. The oldest mention of Cracow comes from 965. The name of the town is inscribed in the Arabic alphabet by a Spanish merchant, Ibrahim ibn Yaqub, and can be pronounced in Polish as *Karako* or *Krakua*. The marriage of the Bohemian princess Dubravka with the prince of Polanie, Mieszko, who had his seat in Gniezno in Wielkopolska, tied the fate of Cracow with Poland. The establishing of a Latin bishopric in 1000 strengthened the position of Cracow, and King Bolesław Śmiały chose Cracow as his base. His successor Włodzisław Herman minted coins with the inscription *Cracov*. When Bolesław Krzywousty, the son of Włodzisław, divided Poland in his last will among his sons, he appointed Cracow to be the seat of the oldest of the brothers.

What did the city look like in those days? On the top of the Wawel Hill, there used to stand a Romanesque cathedral, a stonework royal court, and a town built in stone and wood and surrounded by a rampart. North of the hill there lay Okół – an independent urban settlement with two Romanesque churches of St Idzi and St Andrew, but the whole place was burnt down in 1241 during a Tartar invasion. Two years later, Bolesław Wstydliwy became the ruler of Małopolska. Twenty-six years of his reign brought Cracow peace and ambitiously planned growth. On the 6th June 1257, the duke issued a charter authorising the founding of a town Cracow. The 13th century was the birth of Cracow's Gothic architecture. Unlike the Romanesque stonework, the bricked Gothic buildings have survived until today and give the city an individual character also allowing us to imagine the appearance of the place in times past. In 1287, the town was protected by a rampart, which saved it from the subsequent Tartar invasion. At the turn of the 13th century, it witnessed the struggle to revive the Polish Kingdom. In 1295, Przemysł II was crowned in Gniezno as the king of Poland. For a few years after his death, the country was ruled by Bohemian kings. Władysław Łokietek reinstated the Piast dynasty to the Polish throne by taking over Cracow in 1306, quenching the unrest among its citizens in 1312 and crowning himself at Wawel Cathedral in 1320. This was also his burial place after his death in 1333. Ever since, the Cathedral served as the coronation church and the necropolis of the Polish rulers. The town's rapid development lasting 230 years began with the reign of Casimir the Great (1333-1370). King Casimir founded the university in 1364, and erected a fortified town of Kazimierz (named after him) on the other side of the Vistula, which in time merged into one with Cracow. His granddaughter Jadwiga gave her jewellery for the purpose of refurbishing the university, and by marrying Jagiełło, the Duke of Lithuania, she started a new dynasty on the Polish throne. The rule of the House of

Cracow. Facade of St Mary's Church.

◄ *View of the Main Town Square in Cracow.*

Cracow. Altar pentaptych by Veit Stoss in St Mary's Church.

the Jagiellon was a time of military might and material prosperity for Poland and Cracow. The Cracow Academy flourished during the late Middle Ages and attracted students from all over Central Europe. Nicholas Copernicus studied here between the years 1491 and 1495. The arrival of Humanism followed by Renaissance thought in the early 16th century shaped the character of a hundred year long period, later known as "the golden age of the Polish culture". In 1525, Albrecht Hohenzollern, the last Grand Master of the Teutonic Order, and the first Duke of Prussia, paid tribute to King Sigismund the Elder in the Cracow Town Square. The king erected a magnificent residence in Wawel: a Renaissance court that represents a masterpiece in architecture of the period. The city was a multinational mixture of Poles, Germans, Jews, Italians and Hungarians. The inhabitants occupied highest positions at the court regardless of their origins and nationality. The spontaneous development of printing made Cracow famous and strengthened the role of the Polish language.

The misfortunes brought upon Poland by Sigismund III Vasa were also a blow for Cracow. After the transfer of

Cracow. Western facade of the Cloth Hall in the Main Town Square.

Cracow. Juliusz Słowacki Theatre and statue of Aleksander Fredro.

Cracow. Tent Room II, collection of armour: part of the exhibition in Czartoryski Museum.

the capital from Cracow to Warsaw, the tradition of coronations in Cracow Cathedral still augmented the city's importance. However, the Cathedral got seriously damaged during the two Swedish wars of 1655-1660 and 1703-1721. After the second partition of Poland, Tadeusz Kościuszko, a national hero, arrived in Cracow on the 24th March 1794 driven by the intention of defending Polish independence and announced himself the dictator of a national uprising. After the fall of the insurrection, the royal jewels kept in the Wawel Treasury were plundered by the Prussians. The Napoleonic Wars left Cracow untouched, and the Vienna Congress (1815) decreed the creation of Cracow Commonwealth (*Rzeczpospolita Krakowska*) – a miniature country administered by Poles. The whole of the 19th century represented a period of Cracow's increasing importance in Polish intellectual and artistic life. The university gradually recovered its acclaim: Karol Olszewski and Zygmunt Wróblewski were the first scientists to distil oxygen and nitrogen from condensed air. The National Museum established in 1879 acquired a collection of paintings and sculptures, including the vast canvasses by

Cracow. Bird's-eye view of Wawel Hill.

Jan Matejko. The Czartoryski Museum opened access to priceless national memorabilia and a family-owned collection of art, which contained masterpieces of artists such as Rafael Santi (his *Study for a Portrait* went missing during World War II), Rembrandt van Rijn *Landscape with the Good Samaritan*, and Leonardo da Vinci *Lady with the Ermine*.

On the 6th August 1914, Cracow was the place of departure for the Polish legions of Józef Piłsudski marching off to fight for Polish independence. After Poland regained its freedom, Cracow became Poland's fourth urban centre after Warsaw, Lodz and Lvov. The nightmare of World War II brought the annihilation of the Jewish population, which had always been permanently present in Cracow. The post-war period was predominantly a time of great efforts to try and retain the city's historical heritage. Due to the industrial developments, acid rain began to occur and ruin the memorials of the past at a terrifying pace. The whole Polish community participated in a rescue operation of these sites. In 1978, Cracow was added to the UNESCO Heritage List as one of the twelve most precious architectural complexes in the world. In the same year, the Archbishop of Cracow Karol Wojtyła was elected as Pope John Paul II.

With regard to the number of visitors, Cracow is an absolute leader in Poland. As a city of arts and science it successfully competes with Warsaw. Every second postcard sent from Cracow represents an image of the Gothic Church of the Assumption of the Holy Virgin Mary, more commonly referred to as the St Mary's Church (*Kościół Mariacki*). Its interior holds the most valuable treasure of late medieval sculpture in Europe: the Altar-

piece of Veit Stoss. Born in Nuremberg, the artist came to Cracow around 1477 in order to produce the main altar commissioned by the citizens. The polyptych is made of limewood and consists of a main part and four wings, two of which are visible after the altarpiece is closed. The central scene at the lower part presents the Holy Virgin Mary's Dormation surrounded by large-scale figures of the Apostles (St Peter, who is holding the Holy Mary measures 280 centimetres).

Cracow. Pope John Paul II greeting people from the legendary window of the Bishops' Palace at 3 Franciszkańska Street.

Cracow, Wawel Cathedral. Royal tombs of Sigismund the Elder and Sigismund-August in the Chapel.

Pearl of the Czartoryski Museum: Leonardo da Vinci, Lady with the Ermine.

Royal Castle in Wawel. Tapestry and the throne chair from Sigismund-August's collection.

103

◄ *Salt mine in Wieliczka. Chapel of the Blessed Kinga, carved out in rock salt at the depth of 100 metres.*

Wieliczka. Main altar in the Chapel of the Blessed Kinga.

Wieliczka. Chandelier in the Chapel of the Blessed Kinga made of salt crystals.

Wieliczka

According to the legend, salt came to Poland in the trail of the Hungarian princess Kinga, who married the prince Bolesław Wstydliwy – later the king, who gave Cracow municipal rights. The works that Kinga commissioned in Wieliczka near Cracow did indeed lead to the discovery of rich salt resources, which from the 13th century onwards constituted one of the major sources of income for the Polish monarchs. The mine in Wieliczka was in continuous use until the 1990s. Some of the old mining headings have been converted into an underground museum, and some have been adapted to hold a sanatorium, which makes use of the therapeutic qualities of the microclimate created deep below the surface of the earth in the salt chambers. The effort required to get in and out of the mine was so great in times past that the workers used to spend a whole week underground to avoid the everyday climb of several hundred metres. Therefore, the underground dwellings were provisioned with objects of everyday use. People whose lives are put at risk on an everyday basis by their occupation, often tend to turn to God. This religious devotion motivated the miners to create an unprecedented structure in the salt mine – the Chapel of St Kinga – a temple carved out in salt and located a hundred metres below the earth. All decorative reliefs are made of salt. The salt walls, ceiling and floors are illumi-

Wieliczka. Chamber in the historic salt mine.

nated by huge chandeliers adorned with salt crystals of diamond-like clarity. The underground tourist route, leading through the former mine galleries, is dotted with several similar attractions, although they are smaller in scale.

106

Pieskowa Skała

Pieskowa Skała. Rock formation known as the "Hercules Club".

The Vistula River cuts through Cracow and divides the southern incline of the Carpathian Foothills from the Jurassic range of hills on the Cracow-Częstochowa Upland. Dotted around the hills, along the border with Silesia, there is a chain of castles built by King Casimir the Great between 1333 and 1346 in order to protect the country from the invasions of the Bohemian ruler John of Luxemburg. Little forts perched on rocky cliffs, called "the eagle's nests", were positioned in such a way so that each of them would have the two neighbouring forts within sight. Light signalling between the forts created a system which operated like a medieval telegraph. Signals received from Ojców, which in turn received signals from the Wawel Castle, would be transmitted north by the stronghold in Pieskowa Skała. The latter is situated 25 kilometres from Cracow. It houses a branch of the National Art Museum of Wawel. The location of the fortress, from a strategic point of view, is phenomenal. It surmounts a cliff with a sheer drop on three sides. From 1377, the castle was the seat of the Szafraniec family. It was granted to them as an apology gift from King Louis the Hungarian for some insult to Piotr (*Piesiek*) Szafraniec made by one of the royal soldiers. In the 16th century, the task of rebuilding the structure was undertaken by Hieronim Szafraniec, the secretary of King Sigismund the Elder. The works conducted in stages between 1542 and 1580 were completed with excellent results. It is now the most beautiful 16th century magnate residence in Poland.

Renaissance castle in Pieskowa Skała.

The main nave of the Pauline church in Jasna Góra, Częstochowa.

Częstochowa. Jasna Góra. View of the sanctuary.

Częstochowa

This large industrial city, situated on the border between the regions of Małopolska and Silesia, is known to be "the Catholic heart of Poland". From 1382 there has existed a Pauline Monastery in Jasna Góra, which was rebuilt and fortified in the 17th century, shortly before the Polish-Swedish war. The chapel adjacent to the church holds the famous icon of the Black Madonna. The many blessings bestowed here since medieval times, have made Częstochowa the largest pilgrimage site in Poland and one of the major sanctuaries dedicated to the Holy Virgin Mary in Europe. The last decade of the 20th century saw an annual influx of between three and a half and seven million visitors. August is the peak season for pilgrimages, particularly on the Day of the Assumption of the Holy Virgin Mary (15th August), and a local celebration day of the Holy Mary of Częstochowa (26th August). The number of visits to see the icon of the Black Madonna multiplied after the year 1655, when the

◀ *Częstochowa. Jasna Góra. The Holy Mary of Częstochowa Chapel interior.*

Pilgrims filling the bailey of Jasna Góra.

"The Black Madonna" – icon held in Jasna Góra Sanctuary, an object of worship for Polish Catholics. ▶

monastery "miraculously" withstood the siege of the Swedes. This led to the rise of the whole country, by then nearly totally subjugated by the Swedish army, to oppose the enemy. It allowed King Jan Kazimierz to return to Poland from exile in Silesia. Ever since then, the Holy Mary has been referred to by all Polish Catholics as "the Queen of Poland", and many of the walking pilgrimages to visit her icon cover distances of many hundred kilometres. The oldest of these is the Warsaw Pilgrimage, which has been organised since 1711, and extends over 245 kilometres one way. The attendance in the walking groups is very impressive. In 2001, the Warsaw group alone was made up of over 12,000 pilgrims. Ten years earlier, the total number of travellers arriving at the Sanctuary surpassed 400,000 people.

110

Gołoborze. Unique rock formation, characteristic of the main range of the Świętokrzyskie Mountains.

The Świętokrzyskie Mountains. Towers of the castle in Chęciny.

The Świętokrzyskie Mountains

Stretching between the Vistula and the Pilica rivers, the Świętokrzyskie Mountains are the lowest mountain chain in Poland. Their highest peak Mt Łysica is merely 612 m, but from the naturalist's point of view they are exceptional. They are Poland's oldest mountains. They form a sequence of short mountain ranges overgrown by forests, and surrounded by farmland and industrial terrains. They constitute an unpolluted shelter for nature amongst an otherwise human-dominated environment, and therefore they play an important role in ecological research. The highest range Łysogóry is a protected area and has been included in the Świętokrzyski National Park, which also encompasses fragments of neighbour-ing mountain ranges. Covering 7,632 hectares, the sur-face of the park is 95 percent forest. Fir used to be the dominant tree type, however due to its vulnerability to the effects of human civilisation it was on the brink of extinction. The number of trees had been gradually falling until the 1990s, when the park authorities report-ed an increase of naturally developed fir seedlings. The forests of the Łysogóry range are characterised by the widest variety of tree species in Poland (35). The geo-logical history of the mountains is also fascinating. Palaeontologists have discovered here fossils of species not to be found elsewhere on Earth.

Facade of the monastery in Święty Krzyż.

Święty Krzyż. Altar containing relics of the Holy Cross Timbers.

Święty Krzyż. Frescos representing a Hungarian Prince Imre, who brought the relics to Poland.

Święty Krzyż

The name of the mountain range (literally Holy Cross) is derived from the relic – a bit of timber from the rood on which Jesus Christ was crucified. It is kept in the Benedictine Abbey situated on the second highest peak of the Łysogóry, Mt Święty Krzyż, (595 m), also known as Łysa Góra. Around the mountain top there are stone circles dating back to the days of a pagan cult, which was present in the area in ancient times. In the 4th and 5th century AD, there existed ironworks at the foot of the hill, which supplied iron to the Barbarian tribes harassing Rome. These ancient traditions of smelter are cultivated by the festival of archaeology and folklore, the so-called "Dymarki Świętokrzyskie" in Nowa Słupia. The first church and monastery were built at the top of Mt Łysa Góra in the 12th century and were funded by King Bolesław Krzywousty. The Timber of the Holy Cross relic was brought here the following century. The practically Baroque, architectural complex conceals within its walls relics of Romanesque and Gothic buildings (in the mid-15th century a Gothic church was founded here by the King Kazimierz Jagiellończyk and Cardinal Zbigniew Oleśnicki). The Benedictine Abbey in Święty Krzyż is linked to early examples of Polish medieval writing. The first of these is the Latin Świętokrzyski

Annals (*Rocznik świętokrzyski*) from the 12th century. The other one is known as Świętokrzyskie Sermons (*Kazania świętokrzyskie*), and constitutes a masterpiece of Polish prose style representing the state of the language at the turn of the 13th century. The latter was found in St Petersburg in 1890 in the form of a manuscript, which had been taken away from the Abbey after its liquidation in 1818. Between the years 1825 and 1845, the monastery served as a prison. After World War II it was given back to the clergy.

Trail leading from Nowa Słupia to Święty Krzyż is one of the most difficult routes in the Świętokrzyskie Mountains.

Święty Krzyż, gate to the monastery.

Kazimierz Dolny, view of the Town Square from Mt Trzech Krzyży.

Kazimierz Dolny

"A magical place and a mecca for artists" would define Kazimierz Dolny well. Situated at the narrowing of the Vistula valley, the town used to be one of the most important river ports in Poland. It was founded in the 12th century by the Duke of Sandomierz, Casimir the Just. In the mid-14th century, King Casimir the Great erected a castle here protecting an important trading hub. Since then, there had existed a large Jewish community in Kazimierz (Casimir the Great was their greatest protector). The Jews of Kazimierz were murdered during World War II, but their historical presence left its indelible imprint on the local architecture and the regional cuisine. One of the famous valleys surrounding the town conceals a *kirkut* – a Jewish cemetery. Fragments of tombstones destroyed by Nazis were built into a monument created after the war. Until the 17th century, Kazimierz was the most important point for grain transportation from southern Poland and western Ukraine, as here the cargo was reloaded onto the river boats heading for Gdansk at the mouth of the Vistula. During the Swedish

Kazimierz cockerel, nationally renowned product of the bakery in Kazimierz Dolny.

Town Square in Kazimierz Dolny, burgher houses of the Przybyła Brothers: St Nicholas and St Christopher.

Mannerist House of the Celej Family at Senatorska St no.11, seat of the Nadwiślańskie Museum.

wars the town was destroyed, and by a whim of nature, the valley of the Vistula shifted away from the town by several hundred metres. This brought an end to the commercial life of the place and cut off the source of the local wealth. As a consequence, Kazimierz was "mummified" in this state until the 20th century, when it was re-discovered by artists in search of attractive painting grounds. And indeed, Kazimierz and its environs offer fabulous scenery encompassing nearly all styles of old-time architecture and all types of Polish landscape concentrated within 6-7 km radius. The local museum has four large branches (an absolute record breaker with regards to the per capita statistics for Poland), including the unique Museum of Goldsmithery also exhibiting Judaic objects of art. The whole architectural complex is listed. The most precious buildings include the parish church of SS John the Baptist and Bartholomew, built in a Renaissance style but on Gothic foundations, with a beautifully ornamented interior and the oldest, complete, 17th century organ. Also notable are Mannerist facades of the Przybyła Brothers' Houses, the House of the Celej Family, and the Franciscan church and monastery complex with

View of the parish church from Kazimierz Dolny Town Square.

◄ *Historic synagogue, one of reminders of the once large Jewish congregation in Kazimierz Dolny.*

the wooden steps of penance (to be ascended on the knees).

Residential villas prevail in the town's architecture. All new designs have to be approved by the conservation officer. Permanent residence is most often granted to artists: painters, actors and writers. The tourist season lasts all year round, but the summer offers additional cultural events such as the Film Festival and the Festival of Folklore. During the summer weekends, half of Poland and all of Warsaw's population descend on Kazimierz, but the spring, winter and autumn are ideal for connoisseurs of beauty. During Christmas time, the town's inhabitants stage the Nativity mystery play with their own script and with residents of merit dressed up as angels and shepherds. The produce of the local bakery is known nationwide, especially the "cockerels" made from delicate wheat dough. The town is also well known for its cityscape paintings sold in permanent and temporary galleries.

Ruins of Casimir the Great's Castle.

Lublin. A neo-Gothic prison erected in the early 19th century in place of a former castle (but still known as the Castle), nowadays houses the Lublin Museum.

Lublin

The main city of the Lublin Upland has some 350,000 inhabitants and is situated on the former Polish-Ruthenian borderland. In the 12th century it became the seat of town administrator (*kasztelan*) and protected the eastern borders of the Sandomierz Province. In 1280 it fell into the hands of the Halicz dukes, to whom some sources attribute the laying of the foundations of the stone castle. In 1317, under the reign of Władysław Łokietek, the town was granted the municipal charter. In the mid-14th century, Casimir the Great erected a castle, of which only relics now survive. The town's growth was accelerated by the formation of a trading route connecting the ports of the Black Sea with the Baltic. In 1569, the last Jagiellonian king, Sigismund-August held a session of the *sejm* here, during which a union was signed joining the Grand Lithuanian Duchy and the Polish Crown into one political body (which in the context of the European Union, would seem to be an admirable example of political amity between neighbouring countries). Between the years 1578 and 1795, Stefan Bathory chose Lublin for the seat

Castle courtyard. Elements of medieval construction are preserved in the neo-Gothic wings of the building.

of the Crown Tribunal (the highest law court) of Małopolska, which meant that for the duration of the annual visits of the monarch it served as a "seasonal" capital city. It performed the function of the capital on two other occasions. Firstly, between the 7th and 11th November of 1918, when Ignacy Daszyński formed in Lublin the first government of Poland reborn after the period of partitions. And later, between July 1944 and February 1945, when Stalin installed a Communist gov-

Attic of a Mannerist house belonging to the Konopnic Family (Town Square no.12) in Lublin.

The Chapel of the Holy Trinity near the courtyard, historically and architecturally the most precious element of the castle.

Lublin Old Town: Trinitarian Tower.

ernment here Contemporary Lublin is an important academic centre with two universities the Maria Skłodowska-Curie University and the Catholic Lublin University, set up in 1918, the Technical University, the Medical Academy, the Academy of Agriculture and others. The driving force of the academic environment in the 1960s and

Picturesque lane.

Lublin. Dominican Church of St Stanisław.

"Fire of Lublin". Painting in the Dominican Church depicting the event of 1575.

1970s allowed for the creation of an alternative theatre movement, focused around the festival *Konfrontacje*. From the Middle Ages until the war, Lublin was also an important centre of Jewish learning and philosophy. The first Yeshiva – rabbinical academy – was created here in 1518, and in 1567 received the royal privilege. In 1559 the first Polish edition of Talmud was issued by one of the Lublin presses. Strong traditions of Jewish education continued until the 20th century. In 1930 a new academy was established, Yeshiva Hachmei Lublin, or the Academy of Lublin's Sages. Its founder, Meir Shapiro (1887–1933), was hoping for it to become the world's main rabbinical academy. At the time, the Jewish inhabitants constituted 35 percent of the city's populace. After 1939, the Germans created a ghetto in Lublin, and the Jews were gradually transported to concentration camps in nearby Sobibor, Treblinka and Majdanek and murdered. The image of Lublin crowded with groups of Jewish scholars survived only in literature. The memory of the city's multicultural past is cultivated by the Grodzka Gate (*Brama Grodzka)* centre, situated in the building created in the former city gate near the castle.

Richly ornamented dome of the Dominican Church.

The historic centre still possesses many valuable buildings by acclaimed architects, such as Giovanni M. Bernardoni, Franciszek Koźmiński, Dominik Merlini or Antonio Corazzi. Renaissance, Baroque and Classicist clerical complexes neighbour with burghers' houses. Remains of ancient structures are preserved in the walls of the pseudo-Gothic prison, known as "the castle", built in 1823-26 on the ruins of a medieval fort according to the design by Ignacy Stompf. Byzantine paintings on the walls of the Gothic Holy Trinity Chapel constitute a unique feature of world importance. They were commissioned by the King Władysław Jagiełło in 1395-1418, and symbolise the cultural borderland of East and West.

The Great Town Square in Zamość. In the foreground, the Town Hall combining elements of Renaissance and Baroque.

Zamość

Zamość is a dream come true, a utopia, which has been allowed to exist in our world. This *cita ideale* – the perfect city, was built in accordance with the concepts of Italian Renaissance architecture, with which the author became familiar during his studies in Padua. Jan Zamoyski, as that is his name, was born in 1542 as a son of a noble man of average wealth, the owner of three villages and a little castle in Skokówka. The Zamoyski family came from the west in the Wielkopolska region and was represented by the *Jelita* coat of arms. The first member of the family to be called "Zamoyski" acquired the village Zamość situated in the Lublin Province (today known as Stary Zamość), from which the surname was derived. His name was Tomasz Zamoyski, the great grandfather of Jan.

Angel on the house's facade.

The Zamoyski family earned their status in the neighbourhood thanks to their diligence and hard work. Jan's father, Stanisław became a *starosta* (literally, "elder", an administrative official) of Bełskie province. In his care

for his son's personal and political development, he sent the thirteen year old to the French royal court to educate him in etiquette and the ways of the world. In Paris, Jan Zamoyski undertook studies at both existing universities: the Sorbonne dedicated to scholastic thought and the modern Royal Collegium. After a short visit home, he continued his education in Strasburg, followed by Italy. He returned to Poland as an excellent lawyer and orator, and started an incredible career dedicated to his homeland and to his family's good name as the royal secretary. He inherited his father's title of *starosta* of Bełskie. The king's childless death created confusion in the country and allowed Zamoyski to reveal his political talents. He was the first one to redraft the rules of conduct during interregnum in his province, which were later adopted in whole Poland. As a political leader of the middle nobles, he influenced the election of three subsequent monarchs: Henry of Valois, Stefan Bathory and Sigis-

Zamość. Front of the Great Town Square with houses restored in 1968-82.

Emblem representing the Holy Mary trampling a dragon – decoration on one of Zamość houses.

mund III Vasa. The first one granted him the authority over the Knyszyńskie province in the role of *starosta*, the second one nominated him the the Great Crown Commander-in-Chief and the Great Crown Chancellor, and the third one disappointed his hopes by collaborating with the Habsburgs to the detriment of the Polish state, whose needs were better understood by Zamoyski.

In April 1580 the terrains of Skokówka were designated for construction work of Nowy Zamość. The planning of the new town on this previously undeveloped land was entrusted to an Italian architect Bernardo Morando. The works stared in 1585 and lasted until 1619. Zamoyski did not live to see the end of it, as he died in 1605. He left to his inheritors 11 towns and over 200 privately owned villages. Moreover, he governed royal estates consisting of 12 towns and 612 villages, which combined made up a total of 17,500 km² of land (nearly 60 per cent of today's territory of Belgium).

The location of Zamość near a trading route linking the two large commercial centres of Lublin and Lvov secured the town's chances to develop successfully. The founder's expectations became fact. The final effect was a defensive town, surrounded by seven bastion fortifica-

Zamość. Collegiate church.

Zamość. Synagogue.

Zamość. Interior of the collegiate church.

tions, with five gates (the Lubelska Gate was bricked over after Maximillian Habsburg walked through it as a prisoner of war), with a regular plan of streets, three town squares and the castle of the Zamoyski family (in place of the old little castle) included into the town. The town's population was provided with Renaissance houses with beautifully decorated facades. The first Town Hall was rebuilt in 1639-56 from the original building by Bernardo Morando. Being a fortress, the town also had an armoury. The spiritual needs of the inhabitants were satisfied by churches, the most sumptuous of which, the collegiate of Our Lord's Resurrection and St Thomas, became the final resting place for the founder and his descendants. The stuccowork in Zamoyski Chapel was made in 1634 by Giovanni Battista Falconi. As a commercially driven place, Zamość had its gates open to Armenian and Jewish settlers. The initial urban planning included an Armenian Orthodox church as well as a synagogue. The intellectual development of the inhabitants was to be secured by their own university. Jan Zamoyski founded it in 1595 and named it the Zamojska Academy. However, it was *de facto* on a par with Jesuit colleges. The new building was built in 1639-48. The school was well known for the high level of education it provided, but was never transformed into a fully-fledged college. The right to the academy title was taken away by the Austrians after the first partition of Poland.

Zamość was not the only town built by Jan Zamojski. Other places indebted to him for their existence are situated in Podolia (today in the Ukraine): Szarogród, Skinderpol, Busza, Jangród, Raszków, Jampol (rebuilt with its castle after the war) and a little town and castle in Komarowo. Apart from Zamość, the commander-in-chief built on his Lublin estates Jelitowo, which is today Tomaszów Lubelski. These towns, however, did not have the good fortune to survive in an equally good state.

Nowadays, Zamość is the only Renaissance town in Europe with a fully preserved urban layout and buildings characteristic of the epoch. The town's historical sites have undergone a thorough conservation process. The tourist interest has also increased due to the location of Zamość near an important border checkpoint in Hrebenne, as well as the proximity of the picturesque region of the Roztoka National Park.

Łańcut. Residential complex of the Lubomirski and Potocki families, Museum Castle. View from the west side.

Łańcut

This small town situated 20 kilometres east of Rzeszów attracts masses of tourists each year, ostensibly, on the strength of just one building: the castle. The first small castle was built here by the Stadnicki family. The current castle, considered to be the most magnificent in Poland, was built from scratch by the Lubomirski family between 1629 and 1641, in place of the former residence of the Stadnicki. The architect commissioned to carry out the work, most probably Maciej Trapola, designed an excellent structure having a form described in Italian as palazzo in fortezza – a palace within a fortress. He encircled the castle with a system of bastions, thanks to which Łańcut managed to withstand the attack of the Swedes and of George Rakocsi (Prince of Transylvania) during the wars of 1655-60. Repairs after the fire of 1688 and subsequent extension and renovation works added to the construction elements of other styles, such as Baroque, Rococo, Classicist and Biedermeier. From 1817 Łańcut was the property of the Potocki family, who in the beginning of the 20th century contributed to the estate by erecting neo-Baroque stables and a carriage house. After World War II, the castle was turned into a museum known for its unique collection of sledges and carriages. The main bulk of the building is quadrilateral and two-storey high with an internal courtyard and four corner towers. From the north, it is adjacent to the wing of the library and from the south three-wing outbuildings. The interiors are sumptuously furnished and contain marvellous decorations: Baroque stuccowork by Giovanni Battista Falconi from 1641, and Italian and French wall paintings from the second half of the 18th century. The collection includes sculptures of one of the leading Rome-based artists of Classicism, Antonio Canova (1757-1822), who worked for Napoleon I and for the Lubomirski and Stroynowski families. European painting is represented by Italian, German and French artists, and the Polish collection which includes Sarmatian portraits of the 17th and 18th century among other works. Since 1961, every Monday, Łańcut has been hosting a fantastic festival of music.

Łańcut. Southern wing of the castle.

Łańcut. Neoclassical riding stables built in 1828-30 from the design by Ludwik Bogochwalski.

Łańcut. Synagogue.

◄ *Łańcut Castle. Baroque cupola of the tower designed by Tylman von Gameren.*

River rafting down the Dunajec – one of tourist attractions in the Polish Carpathians.

View from Mt Sokolica over the Dunajec Gorge in the Pieniny.

Krupówki. Main street in Zakopane.

The Karpaty Mountains

The Polish Carpathians stretch along the southern borders of the country starting off in the east with the Opołonek summit over the Użocka Pass, until the dip of the Brama Morawska, which marks the division point from the Sudetes Mountains. These are the highest Polish mountains, but geologically the youngest. They originated in the Alpine orogenesis, however, alpine landscapes in the Polish portion of the Carpathians are represented only by the highest range – the Tatras. All Carpathian ranges situated on the Polish side have demarcated tourist routes: footpaths, cycle paths, horse routes and ski runs, as well as didactic trails. Mountain paths are winding, but are usually in good condition. During wintertime they can be extremely snowed in and seasonally impassable. Snow chains are a must when visiting the Polish Carpathians in winter. Exploration on foot is normally unproblematic, provided you adhere to safety measures and set out equipped in the necessary gear, as well as having a degree of fitness suitable for the season and difficulty level. Encounters with bears and wolves are very rare, and adders can be easily passed. More skills are required when visiting the Tatras, where some trails lead over bottomless precipices and can only be completed with the use of additional safety equipment (clamps, chains). Moreover, winters pose an avalanche threat. Mountain

hiking in Poland, a predominantly lowland country, is a popular form of relaxation, but luckily not all trails are equally well-trodden. Apart from its obvious tourist qualities, the picturesque Carpathians also offer the curative powers of its mineral waters, which can sometimes be combined with apitherapy (the medicinal use of honey bee products). This is conducted for example in Krynica, also known as the pearl of Polish spas, with the traditions of hydrotherapy dating back to 1794. Ferrous oxalate treatment can be complemented here by administrating bee's produce from the nearby Kamianna. Mineral waters from Muszyna, situated similarly to Krynica at the eastern foot of the Beskid Sądecki range, belong to the most popular table waters in Poland.

Szczawnica, the town, whose name signifies a source of acid water (*szczawiany*) lies on the western rim of the above range. It is at the same time the final port on the famous rafting experience on the Dunajec River. It is a fascinating water trail, leading along the turbulent mountain river. Over 23 km Dunajec has many turns and cuts through a deep gorge with steep walls of the Pieniny range. The boating trip is manned by qualified raftsmen and the tourists are transported on special rafts, which are stable and resistant to the wild river's whims. The tremendous success of these rafting trips has encouraged

A view of Morskie Oko (Eye of the Sea) and surrounding mountains.

Czarny Staw (Black Pond) viewed from the route up Mt. Rysy.

the inhabitants of other regions in the Carpathians to organise similar attractions on their own rivers (trying to win more tourists over), however, nothing can surpass the wide appeal of the Dunajec. Therefore, each and every region of the mountains tries to offer its own, unique highlights. The Bieszczady provide the chance of horseback journeys on top of very meek mounts of the Hucul breed, which originates from the Eastern Carpathians. The Beskid Niski Mountains lure resilient hikers with deserted paths, which offer long marches and lots of solitude. The Beskid Sądecki Mountains is a land of elegant resorts, The Beskid Śląski offers a network of skiing runs, and the Beskid Wyspowy is famous for its fruit preserves: syrups and jams, and a produce made in the process of alcohol fermentation of plums and distillation (subject of long and totally needless legal disputes...). The Tatra Mountains are undoubtedly the crown of the whole Carpathians, and Zakopane, the capital of Podhale, situated at its foot is the most visited mountain destination in Poland. The town's popularity is not only due to its geographic location. The tourists are attracted to the living folklore of the whole Podhale region, the exquisite regional cuisine and over 150 years of tourist traditions. Podhale highlanders speak a melodious local dialect, which has developed a literary mode allowing for a regional translation of the Bible, a fact of particular significance for the deeply religious locals.

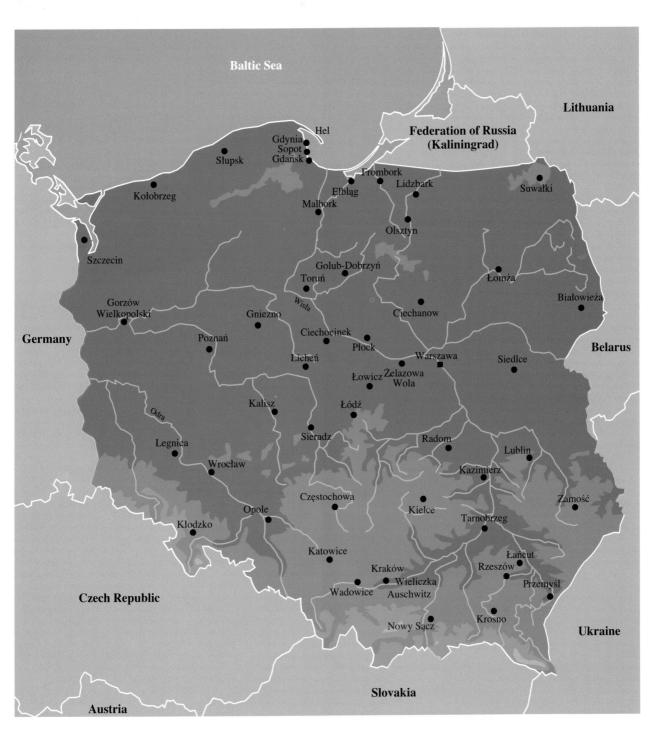

Baltic Sea

Lithuania

Federation of Russia
(Kaliningrad)

Hel
Gdynia
Sopot
Gdańsk
Słupsk
Frombork
Lidzbark
Suwałki
Kołobrzeg
Elbląg
Malbork
Olsztyn
Szczecin
Golub-Dobrzyń
Toruń
Łomża
Białowieża
Gorzów
Wielkopolski
Gniezno
Wisła
Ciechanow
Germany
Poznań
Ciechocinek
Płock
Warszawa
Siedlce
Belarus
Licheń
Łowicz Żelazowa
Wola
Odra
Kalisz
Łódź
Radom
Lublin
Legnica
Sieradz
Kazimierz
Wrocław
Częstochowa
Kielce
Tarnobrzeg
Zamość
Opole
Kłodzko
Łańcut
Katowice
Rzeszów
Kraków
Wieliczka
Przemyśl
Czech Republic
Wadowice
Auschwitz
Krosno
Ukraine
Nowy Sącz

Slovakia

Austria

127

CONTENTS